How to Guide

Writing Better Fundraising Applications

Fourth edition

Mike Eastwood & Michael Norton

DIRECTORY OF SOCIAL CHANGE

Published by
Directory of Social Change
24 Stephenson Way
London NW1 2DP
Tel: 08450 77 77 07; Fax: 020 7391 4804
email publications@dsc.org.uk
www.dsc.org.uk
from whom further copies and a full publications catalogue are available.

Directory of Social Change Northern Office
Federation House, Hope Street, Liverpool L1 9BW
Policy & Research 0151 708 0136; email: research@dsc.org.uk

Directory of Social Change is a Registered Charity no. 800517

First published 1992
Second edition 1997
Third edition 2002
Reprinted 2006
Fourth edition 2010
Reprinted 2012

ISBN 978 1 903991 97 8

British Library Cataloguing in Publication Data
A catalogue record for this book is available from the British Library

Cover design by Kate Bass
Text designed by Kate Bass
Typeset by Keystroke, Wolverhampton
Printed and bound by Page Bros, Norwich

Contents

Acknowledgements iv

Preface v

About the authors vii

Chapter 1   Introduction: what makes a good application 1

Chapter 2   The ingredients of a good application 7

Chapter 3   Building confidence and credibility 23

Chapter 4   Improving your chances 40

Chapter 5   Costing a project 56

Chapter 6   Improving your communication skills 66

Chapter 7   Before you write 77

Chapter 8   Writing a good application 82

Chapter 9   Sending your application 102

Chapter 10   Worked examples 109

Chapter 11   Assessing your application 133

Chapter 12   Checklists and fact files 142

Further reading 157

Index 161

Acknowledgements

We are immensely grateful to Dave Casson for his excellent work on this fourth edition. He has successfully brought his wealth of fundraising experience to bear and the book is all the better for it.

Preface

This is the third edition of the practical guide on how to write good fundraising applications. Since it was first printed in 1992 many funders have come (some have gone), but the key elements of a good fundraising application remain the same. Therefore, the key elements of this book have stayed the same.

The book covers much more than the actual writing of an application. It shows you what information you will need to have available before you put pen to paper – or finger to keyboard – and how to get it. Good fundraising isn't simply about bashing out a stream of letters to possible funders. You need to build your credibility, develop good ideas, marshal the facts and figures you will need, and construct a realistic budget which will not leave you short of money at the end of the day. This book looks at all of that. It also suggests some things to do once you have sent your application off.

Writing applications is an art, not a science. There is no 'identikit' for making a good application. What works well for one organisation, or one fundraiser, may not work for another. So if your current efforts are bringing you the desired results, there is no need to change your style or approach to match the advice given in this book. But there are general lessons which are well worth learning, and it will almost always be possible for anyone to write a better fundraising application.

A good application will not in itself lead to fundraising success. Donors want to know that you are a successful organisation and are able to spend your money cost-effectively on a good project. It is your work they are paying for, not a nicely written and prettily presented proposal. But a good application is one part – and an important part – of a successful fundraising approach.

Occasionally, and this is particularly the case with grants from statutory sources and the National Lottery, you will need to complete an application form. The same principles apply as for writing an application; you simply have less freedom as you are restricted to keeping within the structure of the application form. And you may find that you have to provide a lot more detailed information.

Finally, don't give up easily. Just because you are turned down once does not automatically mean that the application was poor, or the project is unfundable. Learn any lessons you can, and keep at it. Even the best fundraiser doesn't get money every time.

Good luck!

Michael Norton and Mike Eastwood

About the authors

Mike Eastwood

Mike Eastwood is currently Diocesan Secretary in the diocese of Liverpool and Director of Operations for Liverpool Cathedral. He is also a trustee of Merseyside Community Foundation and the Church Urban Fund.

Mike was chief executive of the Directory of Social Change from 1995 to 2001, chair of trustees for the National Association for Voluntary and Community Action, a member of the Advisory Council to the Charities Aid Foundation and a trustee for Liverpool Council for Social Service.

Mike is author of two of DSC's publications: *The Charity Trustee's Handbook* and *Writing Better Fundraising Applications.*

Michael Norton

Michael is founder of the Centre for Innovation in Voluntary Action (CIVA) through which he is currently promoting and supporting a number of projects including MyBank, Otesha UK and FoodWorks. He also runs literacy and library programmes in India.

Michael is the founder of the Directory of Social Change and was its chief executive until 1995. He established Changemakers, is a founder of Youthbank UK and founder and trustee of UnLTD. He also helped to set up UnLtd India, and is currently working on parallel initiatives in South Africa and Canada. He received an OBE in 1998 for services to the voluntary sector.

Michael is widely published and author of three of DSC's publications: *The Worldwide Fundraiser's Handbook, Writing Better Fundraising Applications* and *The Complete Fundraising Handbook.*

1

Introduction: what makes a good application

Fundraising is selling a good idea

You have a good idea, but not the resources (often money) to make it happen. You therefore need to get those funds or other resources from somewhere. Fundraising is about selling your idea to people who have the means to help you make it happen. You have to make them interested in your ideas. And if they are interested enough, they will want to help you. If you are successful, you will get the money, sponsorship or support in kind that you need.

There are many ways of asking. You can ask directly in person. You might make a presentation at a meeting or to a group of potential supporters. You might use the telephone (a key and vastly underrated fundraising aid). You might fill in an application form (online or on paper) or send a written proposal – by post or email.

In practice, the more direct and more personal your approach, the more likely you are to be successful. Many successful fundraisers comment that when they have persuaded a potential funder to visit the project, they have rarely failed to get a donation.

The importance of making a good case

There are many ingredients in a successful fundraising approach: a clear need or problem, a good project, the positive impact of the work, the involvement of users, the credibility of your organisation, the individuals involved in the work and the interest of the person being approached will all be crucial. But it is important to remember that the approach itself is an opportunity for you to make a good case, state your need and ask for support.

A good proposal may not get a bad project funded. But a poor proposal might considerably reduce your chances of success, however good the project. It is important to put forward the best possible case when you have the opportunity to do so. People fail to do this surprisingly frequently, as some of the worked examples in chapter 10 show.

By improving your proposal you will improve your fundraising effectiveness. You are more likely to raise the money your organisation needs – and you will do this with greater confidence, with less effort and at lower cost.

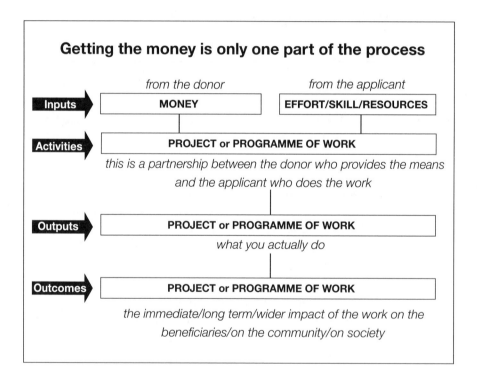

The importance of building good relationships

It is very important when putting together proposals to remember that getting the funds is only one part of the process. It can be helpful to view the process as a whole, as shown in the figure above. There are (at least) two contributors to the project or activities: you (the applicant) and the donor. Without either the project would not happen. Donors have their own priorities and impacts they are aiming to achieve. Keeping this in mind will not only help you to approach suitable funders, but will help you to approach them as partners in the work, not merely sources of money to be forgotten once the cheque arrives. Fundraising is about building relationships.

The key steps in fundraising success

People often try to write an application as a means of working out what they should be doing. This is a recipe for disaster. Good preparation is essential. The more you get ready in advance, the easier and quicker you will find it to write a good proposal. Thinking, planning, discussing, budgeting, re-thinking, re-planning and re-budgeting all take time, but it is time well spent.

Whether you set out your proposal in a brief letter or as a weighty document describing the project in great detail; whether you produce a printed brochure to send out with a covering letter as part of a major appeal campaign or send a direct mail approach to thousands of potential supporters; whether the proposal has to be completed on the donor's own application form or the donor prefers you to explain the project in your own way, the following are the steps you will need to take, once you have an initial idea:

1 **Identify your selling points**
   A few key reasons why the work you are doing is important and why donors will want to support you are the main ingredients of a good application. Remember there is a massive difference between saying what you are doing and stressing why it is important. Research, statistics or figures that help demonstrate the importance of your cause, the extent of the need, the value of the work and the success of your methods should all be used to back up your cause; don't just make assertions. An important selling point is the impact of your work – the changes it will bring to people's lives, the community or the environment.

2 **Build your credibility**
   Get yourself and your organisation known in the grants world, develop effective public relations and get (positive) publicity for your work.

Don't underestimate the value of meeting donors informally. This is often when the best fundraising is done.

Get endorsements and statements from other people that highlight the importance of your work and what you are trying to achieve. These should give the donor an increased confidence in your ability to deliver.

3 Plan your project

Some ideas and projects are so good that they have no difficulty in being funded. Think about your work and see if there are ideas or projects that have a greater chance of attracting support. Be clear about what you intend to do, how and when you will do it and the benefits or outcomes. Develop grant-winning ideas.

4 Cost the project and plan long-term funding

Put together a financial plan, making sure your budget for the project covers all the items of expenditure you plan to incur. Think about how you intend to attract funds for the project both immediately and on a continuing basis (if the project is to continue). Sort out your fundraising strategy – how your organisation is to be funded over the next few years, whether this is realistic and what you need to do to put your organisation's funding on a secure basis.

5 Research and identify likely grant prospects

Avoid the scatter-gun approach. Make carefully targeted approaches to a few funders rather than writing a circular letter to anybody and everybody. Find out what the funder is interested in (particularly why it might be interested in supporting your work) and the scale of support you might expect. Identify any connections between you and the funder. Cross-reference your ideas and projects with likely funders, matching their interests and concerns to your needs. Also, be sure you know which budget the money is coming from. For example, if you are approaching a company, you could be looking for support from the donations budget, corporate PR, marketing or personnel department or even its employee-giving or voluntary committee. Your approach will need to be adapted accordingly. *Target appropriate funders.*

6 Write a good proposal

Write a clear, coherent, forceful and enthusiastic application, making a really good case for support. Indicate as specifically as you can how and how much the funder might contribute.

7 Make the approach

Decide how and who is to make the approach. You may wish to make preliminary contact or enter into informal discussions before you submit a proposal. The funder may also have particular requirements for the submission of applications, which you will need to follow. Increasing numbers of funders are requesting an initial outline proposal form or an expression of interest, which needs to be submitted prior to a full application being completed.

Provide back-up literature. This could include brochures, your latest annual report, case studies of success and other appropriate information that can be attached to your written proposal. These will enhance your case and improve your chances of success.

8 Follow-up

If you succeed in getting a grant or any other support, note any restrictions or obligations on your part and make sure you comply. Say 'thank you' immediately. Maintain contact with those who are supporting you (obviously), but also with those who are not (where you feel they are or should be interested in your work). Report on your successes and continue to build your credibility with them.

Ask those who have supported you for further support next year or the year after, having checked any restrictions – they have already demonstrated that they like you and what you are doing. Go back to those who have turned you down if you feel that they should be interested. Persistence really can pay. Note any reasons given for rejection. It may be worth finding out whether there is a chance of reapplying and trying to fix up a meeting to discuss your proposals further.

The function and purpose of the proposal

When making a proposal to a funder, you will be aiming to:

- raise money (and/or other support) for your organisation and its work. This is obviously your number one objective: to raise as much money as you can from the particular funder you are approaching. You will need to know what level of support the donor is likely to give, and whether you can expect and obtain a regular grant rather than a one-off payment. If you do not raise the most you can from each funder, this is a missed opportunity and will increase the amount of fundraising work you will have to do to create, build and improve your relationship with the funder. Your application should promote your organisation and its work. Whether or not you are successful, the funder will get to know more about you as a result of the approach. Good relationships are the cornerstone of effective fundraising. So even if you are not successful this time, you may have laid the ground for a successful approach in the future.

The ingredients of a successful application

- Your key selling points
- Credibility and endorsements
- Project plan
- Project budget and funding strategy
- Donor research
- Good proposal
- Back-up literature

2

The ingredients of a good application

Your key selling points

Your application has to catch a funder's attention and stand out of the pile as something worth supporting. One of the major grant-making trusts receives thousands of applications and gives about 350 grants a year. The current success rate of the Big Lottery Fund's (BIG) Reaching Communities programme is around 20%.

You need to do more than tell funders what you plan to do. You have to tell them why your work is important and why it makes sense for them to support you. Organisations must believe in what they do and enthuse about their achievements and successes. If you can't be clear and enthusiastic about your work, a potential funder certainly won't be.

You will need to make a number of key points that catch the reader's attention, arouse interest and 'sell' the proposal. For example, what is unique, special and different about the work you are doing? Why is it necessary and important? What will it achieve? What will grab a funder's interest or excitement? Why would the funder want to support it?

You will have limited space to get these points across and you need to use the space effectively. Deciding your key points will help you do this.

Fundraising is much more than just asking for money. Fundamentally, it is about change. You, the fundraiser, need to persuade potential donors that you can change things for the better. They will give you money on the expectation of change.

So how do you do all of this? Here are five points you need to include and others you might consider making.

1 The problem and the need

Voluntary organisations exist to meet important needs (for example, older people being isolated and neglected; young people at risk of crime or abuse; disabled people being discriminated against; the environment being destroyed by overuse and pollution). You must define the problem in words funders can understand and in a way that makes them feel they want to do something about it. If you can't show why it is really important that your work continues and develops, you will not get the money.

BIG's Reaching Communities programme currently has two criteria against which it assesses applications, the first of which states: 'The proposed project outcomes *meet an identified need* and help to achieve the programme outcomes'. Outcomes (see page 14 and onwards) cannot be determined if the need has not been clearly identified and cannot be assessed if the need has not been clearly described. You must show that there is a need for the project and this has been clearly identified.

Try not to generalise. Many applications make bland assertions such as 'we work with young people excluded from school' or 'everybody knows that we have a serious drugs problem among young people and the problem is growing'. You need to do much more. You need to show the following:

- **What is the nature of the problem you are tackling?**
  For example, 'More and more young people are developing long-term health problems through lack of exercise'. Ask yourself 'What are the needs of our users?' (If you're not getting anywhere, try to describe the difficulties or challenges a typical user may have to face.) It should be clear who will benefit and in what way they are disadvantaged (for example, through poverty, ill health, disability or lack of facilities).

- **How do you know the need exists?**
  How has the need been identified? Evidence can come from various sources. You will need to spend time carrying out research to provide evidence. Where possible the most important evidence will come from

the people who will benefit from your work. For example, you may have carried out surveys among the young people in your area; you may have results of other people's research showing the link between lack of exercise in young people and development of long-term health problems.

Evidence of need

This can come from a number of sources:

- your own research or consultation: for example, feedback, surveys and questionnaires. It should involve people with direct experience of the need and potential beneficiaries of the project
- experience and knowledge of the people in your organisation: recent relevant research can be used to back up your own evidence
- relevant local, regional and national statistics: these could be about the general population in your area or the particular group of people you want to benefit.

- **How widespread is it?**
  You need evidence for your claims. For example, 'Over 50% of children aged 11–16 watch more than three hours of television each night. Only 5% regularly do more than four hours' physical exercise each week.'

- **Why is it important?**
  Don't assume that the reader understands the problems you are describing. Spell them out. Stress the importance of what you are doing and why something must be done – now. If you can't, the funder may prefer to turn to someone else who can. For example, 'Already health specialists are warning that this level of inactivity at an early age is storing up serious heart problems for the future. Indeed, as a leading cardiologist recently said: ". . ."'

You can also state the consequences if nothing is done. Show how the situation will get worse and worse as the problem grows more acute. For example, 'The surgical costs alone are expected to double to over £X million a year. This does not take account of the economic costs of increased absence from work owing to ill health.'

- **Are there any social trends which demonstrate that the problem will increase in the next few years?**
  Prevention is usually cheaper than cure; it is certainly preferable. So if you can show how changes in society are likely to make the situation worse, this will add weight to your argument. For example, 'If people do not develop the capacity to take exercise early in life, they can effectively be cutting out a whole series of leisure options later on. As people retire earlier this could have a serious impact on their quality of life in retirement because . . .'

- **Are you building on work you or other organisations do to address the particular need?**
  You should be able to demonstrate how your proposed work builds on existing work and links in to other projects, providing a more complete solution to the needs identified.

If yours is a local project, you will also need to answer the following question.

- **What are the specific features of your area or community that make support for your project particularly important?**
  Not all communities are the same. Why is the need great in your area (for example, no one else is doing anything or a particularly high percentage of young people are excluded from school)?

EXERCISE

Ask yourself the following questions (taken from a major trust's guidelines):

1 What is the need for the work?
2 How have you identified it?
3 Why have you decided to do this work?
4 Who have you consulted about the project/proposal?
5 What did this tell you?
6 How will this work build on your previous activities?
7 What are your links with other organisations doing similar work?

In addressing the question of need, be as specific as you can. Give facts and figures wherever possible. Do not make generalisations or use hollow phrases such as 'urgent problem' or 'desperate need'. One or two key statistics can do more for your case than a page of well-intentioned waffle.

Also, and crucially, all of the above is about the people you are trying to help, not about the needs of your organisation. So many people apply because 'we need a minibus' or 'we need a new building'. At this stage, don't talk about your own needs, stress the needs of your intended users or beneficiaries. Show what difference you (with the help of the funder) can make to their lives.

Lottery (Reaching Communities programme) assessment of need criterion 1

The first judgement point under this criterion states: There is a need for the project and this has been clearly identified.

In assessing whether this has been achieved the following questions are considered:

- whether there is a clearly defined need or needs that the project will address
- whether the applicant has carried out or referenced open and inclusive research and consultation that is recent and relevant to the project and demonstrates a clear need
- whether the consultation has been extensive and detailed and included potential beneficiaries and all relevant stakeholders
- whether the consultation clearly shows that the project will fill identified gaps or add value to existing provision.

---

2 Your proposal

It is not enough to persuade the funder that there is a real and urgent need to be met; you also need to show that you have a sensible and practical solution to the problem. There may be more than one factor contributing to the need and, if so, you must be clear about which factor(s) you are addressing. If there are some factors that you are not addressing you should be able to give clear reasons why. Perhaps someone else is addressing these issues and your work complements theirs.

Again, you should be enthusiastic. The proposal needs to be clear about the activities you will undertake, the services you will provide and the difference those services will make. Try to excite the donor by showing that something positive and effective can be done. Some ways of doing this are listed below.

- **State clearly what you are going to do – inputs and outputs**
  Inputs are the activities you will undertake to deliver the service your project will provide. Outputs are the services the project provides. Don't just say: 'We will work with the relevant agencies to encourage young people to become more active at an early age.' How are you going to do this? You need to be specific. For example (continuing with the health risk example on page 8) you could say: 'We will develop a series of basic training programmes that any young person will be able to follow. They will require only 15 minutes' exercise, three days a week. Much of this can be done alongside existing day-to-day activities.'

- **Do these activities and services address the need?**
  Having clearly defined the need, you must show that what you intend to do (which is what the funder will pay for) actually addresses the defined need. Will the 15 minutes' exercise, three days a week, be sufficient to address the need?

- **Are these activities the best way to address the need?**
  Are there other ways of addressing the problem? You need to give reasons why you have chosen to carry out these particular activities and services. Are the services something the young people will be enthusiastic about – have you asked them? Ideally the activities and services programme will have been drawn up in consultation with potential beneficiaries.

- **How can you guarantee that it will work?**
  You can't! However, you can show what practical steps you will be taking to ensure that there is every chance of success. So: 'Local celebrities – including X Olympic champion – will visit every school and youth club in the area to talk to children and young people about the health risks they run without proper physical exercise. They will hand out the basic training programmes and do a demonstration exercise.

They will follow this up with repeat visits to the schools and clubs. We will also run activity sessions in school holidays in which . . .'

Funders are – or at least appear to be – increasingly risk-averse. The more that you can reassure them that you have the capacity to deliver the intended benefits of the work, the more likely they are to fund you. This is one key reason why so many funders now ask about your management committee. They want to know that committee members have a good range of professional skills or, if not, then they know appropriate people to turn to for help and advice.

Funders don't like to appear to fail. The excellence of your people, their experience of this kind of work, your organisation's overall track record – these are all important factors in convincing funders that their money will be well spent through you (more on this in chapter 3). Try to give the funder a clear plan of action, including numbers involved and where, when and how it will all happen.

EXERCISE

Ask yourself the following questions (again as given in the guidelines of a major trust):

1   What will the funding support (inputs)?
2   What activities are planned (outputs)?
3   Where will they take place?
4   How long will they take?
5   When will they be completed?
6   What do you want to achieve through the work and who do you aim to reach?

3 Your effectiveness

Many funders have previously been supporting activities (a service, building or whatever), rather than improvements in people's lives. However, the move to funding outcomes means that, instead of funders giving support based on your activities, they now give support based on what your activities achieve. You need to be clear about what the outcomes of your work are and how you will know that they have been achieved. You should cover the following points:

- **State clearly the difference your project will make – outcomes**
  The outcomes are the difference the services you carry out will make to the people or organisations your project will benefit. Funders are increasingly taking an outcomes approach in assessing which projects they will support. In 2003, the then Community Fund stated: 'We intend to put a greater emphasis on outcomes. This means that organisations and groups that we fund will have to demonstrate that they are making a measurable short-term difference and contributing to making a long-term difference to the lives of people they seek to help.' This approach has been developed further by the BIG Reaching Communities programme, which now assesses applications using only two criteria, the first of which states: 'The proposed project outcomes meet an identified need and help to achieve the programme outcomes' (i.e. the BIG Reaching Communities' own outcomes).

For example, a funder does not fund a salary (input) or an advice service (output), but for people to be better informed and make better choices (outcome).

- **Show how you will monitor and evaluate your work**
  Outcome funders, which support the results of your work, expect you to monitor indicators showing that these outcomes have been achieved. You have to be able to show that you will know you are achieving the outcomes. For example, in an employment training project, it is not just the number of people trained that is important, but the number of people who get proper employment as a result – and the number that continue to be in employment after a year. See chapter 4 for more on outcomes.

- **Show that your outcomes match the funders' outcomes and priorities**
  Funders usually have their own aims and objectives, what they would like to see achieved with their support. Once you have established the outcomes of your proposed work, you need to identify funders that are working to the same priorities. You should define your outcomes first, not try and bend your outcomes to those of a funder from which you think you can get support.

- **Demonstrate that your work is effective**
  Do you have a good track record? Have you gone from strength to

strength? Or at least, have you done one thing really well? Can you show that you have achieved positive results before? If so, what were they and why were they so great? Can you get a supportive quote from someone whom the funder will respect?

In fundraising terms, success breeds success. Indeed many funders, when considering your application, ask themselves: 'What does the history of this organisation say about its likely future?' If you simply lurch from crisis to crisis, they may assume that you will never be able to work effectively and efficiently. If you are constantly in debt, they will be loath to risk their money on you. However, if you have a track record of breaking even each year, of receiving and managing grants well, of delivering good quality and well-valued work, they will take great confidence from

EXERCISE

Ask yourself the following questions:

1 What will the outcomes of your project be?
2 How will you monitor your work against these outcomes?
3 What evidence will you collect?
4 How will you evaluate your progress?
5 How does your track record demonstrate that your work is effective?

The three Os

Many funders talk in terms of objectives, outputs and outcomes.

- The objective is the aim of the project, what you are trying to achieve (e.g. 'we are aiming to provide a mobile welfare rights advice service, giving specialist advice to low-income families in their own home').
- The outputs are what and how much gets delivered (e.g. 'we aim to provide 25 advice sessions a week').
- The outcomes are the difference your work will make in the short and long term (e.g. 'we aim to help people lead more independent

> lives as they take control over their own income and financial planning').
>
> Make sure that you are clear about the aims, outputs and outcomes of your project. This will reassure funders that you are a well-managed, well-thought-through outfit that would use their money effectively.

all this and your application will be all the stronger as a result.

A very useful and increasingly used tool in thinking about aims, outputs and objectives is the Charities Evaluation Services' Planning Triangle. This enables you to start at any of the three points and think through what you are doing and what it will achieve. The triangle is available on the Charities Evaluation Services' website: www.ces-vol.org.uk (just type 'triangle' into the search field).

4 Cost-effectiveness

In addition to showing that your work will be (and is) effective, you need to demonstrate that it is value for money. You need to show that you represent a good investment, that money spent on your project will give maximum benefit for an appropriate cost. This will mean having answers to the following questions:

- **Can you show that what you plan to do is an efficient and cost-effective way of dealing with the problem?**
  How many people will be helped? How many will use the facilities, at what cost per person and with what results? Ideally, you should be able to show high numbers at low cost. For example, 'The schools' pack will only cost £5,000 to produce but will be used by over 20,000 young people over the next three years.'

  Funders like to know exactly what will happen as a result of their giving money – how many people will be helped, by whom and when. These kinds of outputs are increasingly important in persuading funders that your ideas are well-thought-through and, by implication, effective.

- **Does your work represent value for money and does it compare well (or better) with alternative approaches to dealing with the problem?**
  Showing value for money is increasingly important, especially to trusts

and BIG. They want to make sure that they are getting the maximum benefits from the money they spend.

You could show how much will be saved as a result of your work. For example, drug-related crime costs £X per week and you get, on average, five people a year off drugs. This will reduce the cost of crime by £Y. Alternatively, you may stop people turning to crime; you may prevent environmental decay, stop people staying away from school or prevent people needing expensive medical treatment. You can put a cash value on all of these savings.

You could try to show how your work brings lasting benefits to your users and their families and then put a value on these benefits. For example, if you help people acquire new skills they will have these skills for life and they may become more confident in other areas as a result. They will therefore become more employable, which may turn them from being benefit recipients into tax-payers.

You could try to show that by spending money you will generate money. Your advice sessions, costing £X, may result in several hundred people receiving £Y in unclaimed benefits; you may help people save money on heating bills; you may be able to develop a chargeable service that will underpin your organisation's financial security. Again, you are showing how a small amount of money given to you now would lead to a long-term benefit well in excess of the value of the grant given.

Knowing the effectiveness, impact and cost-effectiveness of your work can help you make a good case. It will also help you manage your project better. Monitoring and evaluation are an important aspect of your work. If you can demonstrate success, people will want to support you.

Not everything has to be done at the lowest cost. You need to balance the quality of your output with the quantity. If you are dealing with special needs which require particular effort, or if you are doing more than just papering over a problem, then this can also be made explicit and turned into a point in your favour. Show how you are getting to the heart of the problem that everyone else is ignoring while the cost of the neglect just grows and grows. However, if your work appears 'expensive', make sure you explain why this is still the lowest realistic cost for meeting this really important need.

5 The involvement of users

It is becoming essential to show funders that your users, the people who will benefit from the work you are trying to get funded, are committed to the ideas you are putting forward. Funders do not like the idea that you assume that you know what's best for your users. Rather, they want to see that your users have been fully involved in helping shape the project plans. This can be done in a number of ways:

- involving users and ex-users in running the organisation. Do you have users or former users on your management committee? If not, do you have people, aside from paid members of staff, who can speak with knowledge and sympathy on behalf of the users?
- involving users and ex-users in running the programme. Will users work or volunteer on the project? Will they be part of the project steering group? Can you prove that the kind of people who will be benefiting from the project's work will also have a say in how it is delivered?
- involving users in drawing up and planning the project. Show that you don't know best and that you are not trying to impose your ideas, but that the plans and ideas have come from those who really know – your users. This can be done through user groups, questionnaires, community surveys and such like.
- involving users and ex-users in the monitoring, evaluation and feedback processes.

Users should be the centre of the planning process; they are not, and never should be, simply an afterthought. Make sure you can prove that your users – or at least their representatives – are fully committed to the project you are proposing.

EXERCISE

Ask yourself the following questions (based on assessment by BIG Reaching Communities programme):

1 Has consultation about the need for the project included potential beneficiaries?
2 Are there appropriate plans to involve beneficiaries fully in planning and delivering the project?
3 Are beneficiaries involved in monitoring and evaluation of the project?
4 Is the organisation reflective of the beneficiaries of the project?

Selling points: an example

A local youth club, for example, will highlight different selling points when appealing to different donors. For example:

1 To the local authority
- You deliver its strategic objectives for young people (e.g. personal development work, diversionary activities for young people at risk).
- You run a 'professional' service using qualified leaders and meeting all technical and other requirements. Previous club members are now trained leaders.
- You are efficient – you attract the correct ratio of young people to session leaders or staff.
- You have excellent child protection procedures.
- You are effective – you run an excellent service.
- There is a need – your catchment area has a high incidence of need and a low provision compared with other areas.
- You lever in support from other sources.
- You are cost-effective and provide value for money.

2 To the parents of local young people
- You provide a 'containment service', keeping young people off the streets and out of harm's way.
- You provide an educational service – your programme of activities is attractive, and young people acquire new skills and interests.
- You take young people to places they otherwise would not be able to get to, or they undertake activities they have never done before.
- You do all this at extremely low cost – only a few pounds per term.

3 To grant-making trusts
- There is a real need and only you are meeting it.
- The outcomes of your project match the priority outcomes of the particular trust.
- Your work is well thought of and you have achieved maximum possible funding from statutory sources.

- The project you are proposing is an interesting development or an innovative approach to dealing with a particular problem. If successful, other groups elsewhere could copy it.
- You are using new media (e.g. arts, sport, IT) for engaging with young people and the particular trust has an interest in this.
- Other trusts have supported you and are continuing to support you.

4 To local companies
- You are keeping people off the streets and from doing harm. The company may then have a vested interest in supporting them on these grounds.
- There are educational, training and work experience benefits – all of interest to companies. Ultimately this will bring them high quality recruits and/or customers.
- You are a well-run and successful local charity, so it makes sense for them to support you, out of a sense of local community responsibility.
- Children of company staff are or have been youth club members – current leaders are company employees.
- The company will get good publicity in the local press in return for the donation – and you have evidence that you have obtained such publicity before.

6 Other selling points

There is a whole range of other key points that you may wish to make.

- Involvement of volunteers. Time is precious. If people willingly give you some of theirs this must be a point in your favour. You may also be giving volunteers transferable skills and training opportunities as well as saving the cost of having to pay people to do the work.
- Your ability to mobilise support in kind. Show that you can think around a problem, that you are not just cash-obsessed.
- Your ability to attract support from other sources – particularly from the statutory sector.
- Your financial security and sustainability in the medium and long term. Show that you are a safe bet.

- The proportion of funds you generate or propose to generate yourselves. Self-help at every level is very attractive to funders.
- The support you get in membership or donations from the local community. Having community support is another strong plus point.
- Collaboration with other organisations. Show how you avoid unnecessary duplication and overlap, and that between you provide a comprehensive service.
- Leverage – that is, being able to demonstrate how a large impact can be produced from a relatively small amount of support. You can also show how the grant will be used to mobilise further support.

All these will be seen as plus points by funders. They will demonstrate that you are resourceful and effective and show funders that their pounds will be well 'invested' with you, creating, as the Americans say, 'more bang for the buck'.

You must be able to come up with several good reasons why your project should be supported. You need to make these the key 'selling points' in your proposal. You may not be able to get all of them into every application, but highlight those that are the most important as well as those that are of specific interest to that particular donor.

It is a good idea to work out your key selling points and then discuss and agree them with your colleagues and your management committee or trustees. These points will be the basis on which you present your organisation when you are seeking support, so it is important that they reflect how people within the organisation see it and its work.

If there is anything you are unhappy with, where you feel that the organisation could be doing better, this is something that you should discuss with your colleagues. Anyone trying to raise money for an organisation must believe that it is doing the best job it can and if there are problem areas – as there often are – that it is doing its best to sort these out.

EXERCISE: YOUR SELLING POINTS

Write down at least three selling points under each of the following headings. Ask other people in the organisation for their ideas.

1 We meet the following need(s) . . .
2 The needs we meet are particularly important because . . .
3 The outcomes of the work will be . . .
4 The following shows that we are effective . . .
5 We are different or unique because . . .
6 Our other strengths are . . .
7 If we did not exist then . . .

Building confidence and credibility

Credibility

Fundraising is as much who you know (and who knows you) as what you know. Indeed, it is sometimes said that fundraising is 10% what you know and 90% who you know. The figures may not be that extreme, but it is important to know and be known. Organisationally you need to be known, liked and trusted. It also helps if you are personally known, liked and trusted.

Some professional grantmakers may have heard of you well before you have discovered them. It is their business to know what is happening and to identify the projects, organisations and individuals that are making things happen. However, don't wait for them to find you. It is your business to get yourself noticed and establish your reputation. Funders will support you because they believe in you and your organisation's ability to run good projects, as much as in the specific project for which you are seeking funds.

Sometimes funders will support you because they have heard about what you are doing and believe in the cause, sometimes because they have come into contact with you, sometimes because of a personal contact or commendation, sometimes because they have heard of the patrons, trustees or prominent people associated with you. All of this can be as important as the quality of your work and the excellence of your written proposal.

Assume that a funder agrees that you have demonstrated a clear and important need and that you have a sensible plan for dealing with the problem. The funder's next question is: 'That's all very well, but how can I trust this lot to deliver on this?'. In many ways this is the key question. There are lots of good ideas around. You need to show, not only that you have a good idea, but that you have the ability to make it happen. You can do this by demonstrating the effectiveness and clarity of your solutions to the problem and by defining clear and achievable outcomes (see next chapter). However, you must also establish your credibility.

You need to show that you have ability and professionalism, that you have support in the community and that you have a track record of success.

Credibility for new organisations

Credibility generally comes with a good track record, but if you are new – or relatively new – you don't really have one. So what can new organisations do to demonstrate their credibility?

- Talk about the expertise of all those involved in the work (some funders ask you to include CV(s) of the project's main worker(s)).
- Show what excellent ideas about, and solutions you have to, the problems you were set up to deal with.
- Show the calibre of people you have as staff, management committee members, patron, vice-presidents, project advisory groups, etc.
- Get letters of endorsement from a range of key people and agencies.
- Demonstrate, by the quality of your business and project planning, that you have seen a clear need, are capable of delivering an effective solution and have thought through a sensible and clear long-term funding plan.
- Show that the project is based on a successful model developed elsewhere, although you have modified it to adapt to the particular circumstances you face.
- Try and get some early press coverage about why the project is needed and what you hope to achieve.

All you are trying to do is give the funder the confidence that you know what you want to do and how you want to do it, that other people think that the project is worthwhile, and that you are confident of succeeding. Doing some or all of the above should ensure you achieve this.

Your ability and professionalism

Show that you are a well-run outfit, that you have grown and developed over the years, that you are soundly financed, that you have a wide support base, that you have qualified and committed staff and that you look after your volunteers with appropriate training or other support. The days of the enthusiastic amateur are by no means over (and hopefully never will be); but the days of the incompetent amateur are numbered.

The Big Lottery Fund's (BIG) *Good Governance Guide* states:

> In order to ensure these [BIG] funds are spent effectively we have a number of measures in place to satisfy us that organisations that receive lottery funding have sufficient and appropriate governance arrangements. We pay as much attention to your organisation's capacity to handle public funds as we do to the project you are hoping to run. We review your application form and the governance arrangements of your organisation as detailed before we assess the project proposal.

This means that funders such as BIG are looking at the way your organisation is set up and run, its policies, procedures, management arrangements and financial controls, as well as relationships with stakeholders, including trustees, staff, volunteers and beneficiaries.

The assessment of applications to BIG's Reaching Communities programme includes the following judgement points:

- The project is likely to achieve the intended outcomes.
- The project is likely to be delivered well.

In assessing these points, these are some of the questions considered:

- Is the organisation financially healthy?
- Are there comprehensive resource plans in place and appropriate levels of support to staff?
- Are there comprehensive procedures in place to manage external relationships and partnerships and does the organisation have a good record of working with other organisations?

In summary:

> We are seeking reassurance that your organisation has sufficiently sound governance to enable you to concentrate upon the delivery of what your organisation has been set up to achieve, which includes the project we will be funding.
>
> (*Good Governance Guide*, BIG).

This is all pretty tough stuff. However, funders are becoming more and more exacting about levels of risk. You need to show that you are a safe bet.

A further question considered by BIG in assessing Reaching Communities applications is: 'Has the applicant identified the main risks involved in delivering the project and will they put in place effective responses?'. Although your organisation should have a risk management policy, increasingly applicants to major funders are being asked to show how this applies to, and will be implemented for, the particular project they want funded.

Your support in the community

Show how you have widespread support and goodwill throughout the community. Such support will strengthen your efforts and create a sense of 'ownership' in what you are doing. The level of support from, and involvement of, volunteers also shows that people are willing to give time and effort to your cause. It may be worth estimating the value of this and other non-cash support, whether or not it forms part of your formal accounts. Also show that your users think really well of your work and how you involve them in the planning and delivery of your services.

Your track record

Show that you have successfully done similar work in the past or that you have set up other projects, which have gone really well. Show how effectively you have been able to spend previous grants. Again, what does the history of your organisation say about its likely future? Does it show that there is nothing unusual in your applying for and receiving funding, spending it well and continuing to develop new and interesting solutions to your users' problems? If so, the funder will feel confident about your organisation.

EXERCISE: ESTIMATING THE VALUE OF NON-CASH SUPPORT

For last year, estimate the following:

Value of items donated in kind

Item	Replacement cost
	£
	£
	£
	£
Total	£

Value of volunteer time

Number of volunteers:
Total hours of volunteer time:
Total value of volunteer time: (at £ . . . per hour)

Remember to include all the volunteer inputs into your organisation including management committee time. You can value volunteer time at the average wage, the minimum wage, the estimated cost of paying for the time or some notional, but reasonable, figure. Whatever method you use, make sure you state clearly how you have worked it out and/or what it is based on.

Value of secondments

Valued on a similar basis to volunteers

Please note: Were gifts in kind, volunteer time or secondments mentioned in your last year's annual accounts? Do they represent a significant proportion of your last year's total income? If the answer to the first question was 'no' and the second question 'yes', what are you going to do about it?

EXERCISE: LIST YOUR SUCCESSES

List six recent successes in your organisation. Get other people in the organisation (project workers, trustees, the accountant, a committed volunteer) to also make lists – the more comprehensive the better.

1

2

3

4

5

6

Building credibility

Here are some things you can do to show your ability and professionalism and your standing and support in the community:

1 Get comments and commendations from users, experts and funders

- Keep copies of any feedback (letters, emails) you receive from grateful clients and users. Use selected parts to make up a 'quotes sheet', where a range of people say really positive things about you.
- Evaluate your work, either internally or through a formal external evaluation, and make a note of the key points from the evaluation which enhance your credibility.
- Ask experts and others to visit you, and ask them to write to you with their impressions of your work. Then ask if you can use selected quotations to endorse your work.
- Some funders may use your project as a case study or good example of work they support. Use these to endorse your work.

2 Get written about or reported in the local, specialist or national press or media

- Keep copies of any press coverage. If you are a national organisation you may want to use a press cuttings agency to send you copies of any coverage you receive.

- Circulate copies (or a collage) of the press coverage you have received to your supporters, potential supporters and key contacts where you think they will be interested.
- Alert supporters to forthcoming media coverage, especially TV programmes and radio phone-ins, and try to ensure that your voice is heard.
- Record any radio or TV coverage you get. It may prove useful as part of a presentation.

3 Keep in touch with existing donors

- Say 'thank you' promptly for any support you have received. The most cost-effective form of fundraising is to keep hold of existing supporters. Research suggests that it is 11 times more expensive to get a new donor than it is to keep a current one. It is surprising how often grant recipients fail even to thank their donors. And if you forget to do so, it can ruin your chances of getting further support. Remember, you are trying to create an ongoing relationship rather than periodically scrounge for money. A standard receipt or one-sentence thank you may not be the best way to develop good partnerships.
- Send progress reports and a final report on the project. You may be obliged to do some of this under the terms of your grant. Show what you have been able to achieve with the funder's money – outcomes as well as outputs and the impact you are having on the lives of individuals.
- Build an informal working relationship with your main donors. If you are at the same conference, introduce yourself. If there is anything you need to know or want to discuss, telephone them – but don't waste their time.
- Ensure that all queries and correspondence are answered promptly and that telephone calls are received competently and cheerfully.
- Suggest a visit if they are in the area, or invite them to an open day or other similar event. And then make sure that the organisation shows itself at its best.
- Send copies of your annual report, and any other literature you produce which you feel will be of interest, even though you are not asking for money now. You want to show the funder that you are committed to building a long-term relationship rather than simply asking for money when the last lot has run out.

4 Make yourself known to potential funders

Much of the above is also relevant to building relationships with potential funders – those people who you believe might be interested in your work and in supporting it now or in the future. Often it will be far better to develop your credibility with potential funders before approaching them for support. This means you need to get together a target list now, including all those you expect to apply to over the next few years. Put them on the list to receive your annual report, press cuttings, invitations to your annual general meeting and evening receptions and whatever else seems appropriate.

When you first contact them on this basis, explain that you are not asking for money now, but that you hope they will be interested in your work and that they might be willing to support you at some point in the future. This does two things:

- it acts as a point of reference when you actually get round to asking for money
- it shows that you are committed to some sort of partnership. You are not one of those who simply asks for cash and is not heard from again until you want more.

You never know, you may even spark an interest in the funders that will encourage them to approach you or even offer you money.

You may have a lot of contacts with the trustees or administrators of funding sources, but not be aware of the extent. Draw up a list of potential funding sources and discuss it with your staff, trustees and patrons and other prominent supporters. Find out who knows whom and discuss with them how such contacts might be mobilised in your support.

5 Bring people into your organisation

You can bring new people into your organisation, people you feel will be useful to you as:

- patrons, vice-presidents
- expert advisers
- members of specialist subcommittees (e.g. events, fundraising)
- trustees.

You need such people as much for their contacts and to enhance your fundraising credibility as for the practical help they can give. Someone with good contacts can save you hours of painstaking reputation building. So, for example, if you want to raise money from local businesses, try recruiting a prominent and popular local businessperson and get him or her to ask on your behalf (as long as you make it quite clear from the start that this is what he or she is expected to do).

Include a list of your patrons, trustees and other prominent people associated with the organisation on your letterhead and website, if you have one.

6 Keep a credibility fact file

Buy a box file to keep all the press cuttings, commendation letters, statements, quotations, evaluations and endorsements, etc. that you could use in your fundraising proposals. Once it is full, start pruning the out-of-date clippings.

Keep with it a summary fact file with the most recent information you are likely to need.

Credibility fact file

Last updated:

List your five greatest successes in the last five years:

-
-
-
-
-

Other recent successes and achievements of the organisation (two or three):

-
-
-

Main financial sponsors:

- government and official sources
- grant-making trusts
- business sponsors
- individual supporters
- prominent patrons and supporters.

Recent press or media coverage:

Financial credibility

You must show that your organisation is secure, solvent and makes good use of its funds. Your accounts, which many donors require a copy of, can give hidden messages, such as:

- you are flush with funds or running a huge surplus, so you don't really need the money
- you are out of financial control, with expenditure consistently exceeding income, so you can't be trusted with money
- you are spending too much on fundraising, administration or travel, wasting the money you are given.

You may have a qualified auditor's report, saying that the accounts do not present a true and fair view of your financial position (in the auditor's opinion). This can be a disaster and you may need to explain the situation and what you are doing about it.

On the other hand, your financial accounts may not fully reflect the extent of your work. This will particularly be the case if you receive a significant support in kind or through volunteers. These inputs may not be included in the financial accounts but they are important (see page 27 to calculate the value of such support.)

If your accounts (as they are currently presented) will make the work of fundraising more difficult, you will need to do something about this before you start. It may often only be a matter of presentation, getting your accountant or auditor to agree to present the figures in a different way, to set aside provisions for future expenditure or to add explanatory notes to the accounts. Or there may be a more fundamental problem, which you will need to address before you can seriously begin the task of fundraising.

However, fundamentally, funders want to know that you can handle money well. For example, assessors for BIG's Reaching Communities programme consider questions such as:

- **Is the organisation financially healthy?**
  This will look at whether you are solvent, whether you have any deficits and whether other sources of income are secure. If you have any deficits you need to be able to explain why they exist and how they are now under control. An increasingly important aspect of financial credibility is your approach to reserves. Reserves are money in the bank (or invested elsewhere) that you can spend on any part of the charity's work or development. A reasonable level of reserves is now seen as a sign of good management, of taking sensible precautions in an increasingly volatile charity world. Most organisations aim to have at least the equivalent of three months' income as reserves. If you have too much in reserves, or it seems too much to a reader, then you need an explanation of why this is so, i.e. they are restricted funds, only available to be spent for a specific purpose; or they are funds being accumulated for a major project which you will undertake when all the funds have been raised (for example, extending a building).

- **Have all the project costs and overheads been identified, accurately worked out and included in the budget?**
  This is covered in chapter 5, but one quick way to judge an applicant's financial credibility is to examine the budget closely. Funders want to know that you have planned your project carefully, taking into account all the costs involved. They do not want you contacting them halfway through the funding period, saying there is a shortfall. If the funds you are applying for will significantly increase your organisation's turnover, any potential funder will want to know that there are there sufficient management controls in place (or planned) to manage the additional funds.

EXERCISE: JUDGING YOUR FINANCIAL CREDIBILITY

Get hold of a copy of your organisation's latest annual accounts. Study carefully the income and expenditure account, the balance sheet and the notes to the accounts. Jot down some of the positive and negative points that emerge from these figures.

On the plus side:

On the minus side:

Main problem areas to explain:

Many funders now ask to see your reserves policy. This is a simple statement (usually a maximum of two sides of A4) that addresses four basic questions:

- Why do we need reserves (for example, to guard against financial problems and to invest in the organisation's development)?
- What level of reserves is appropriate for us (for example, free reserves equivalent to three months' income – or perhaps more)?
- How are we going to build up a reserve within this policy (for example, by allocating £20,000 of our annual surplus to our reserves for the next three years or perhaps through a general fundraising campaign)?
- How will we monitor our progress (for example, through scrutiny by the finance subcommittee, and including a statement in our annual accounts)?

Understanding your weaknesses

A common reaction by someone reading your proposal is to think up all the reasons why they should reject it. Some typical reasons might be:

'There are too many charities already doing the same thing, and we are already funding *** charity.'

'I've never been to . . . (somewhere miles from where the funder is based) . . . and I don't see why we should be spending our money there.'

'I've never heard of them so they can't be doing a very good job.'

'They have run up a huge deficit. I don't see why we should continue to pour money into them.'

'They spend far too much on administration and fundraising.'

'They are extremely rich; they have enormous assets and reserves. So they don't need our help.'

'They are an expensive service. I think we could spend our money more wisely elsewhere.'

'I remember the bad publicity when two members of their management committee resigned.'

'Their work is extremely controversial.'

'They are too political' (meaning they campaign a lot or are too left-wing or right-wing).

'It sounds like work that should be funded by statutory sources.'

You need to be aware of the potential problems or difficulties people may raise relating to your organisation. Different donors will be concerned about different things. For example, a company may be looking for a clean image, whereas a grant-making trust and BIG will want to know that they are not paying for a lost local authority grant. You need to get inside the minds of the donors and address their concerns accordingly.

When you look at your organisation and its weaknesses, there may be a perfectly good explanation for most of the apparent problems. You then have to decide whether to confront the issue head-on by mentioning the 'problem' and giving an explanation in your proposal, or whether just to have a satisfactory answer prepared in case you are ever asked a question about it. It is not sensible simply to forget that the 'problem' exists.

Often, your fundraising is done through a letter with supporting materials. There is usually no meeting and no opportunity to discuss matters in more detail at a later stage. Therefore it is usually best to try and neutralise any of the possible objections within the letter. This requires careful writing. You do not want to be as clumsy as to say: 'you [the funder] might be thinking "gosh this is really expensive". Let me show you how is isn't.' Rather, you should explain that the cost of dealing with the problem is X. This is much more cost-effective than the conventional Y approach, and is certainly much cheaper than the Z cost of not doing anything at all. Or, that you are dealing with a particularly vulnerable group or intractable problem that requires a great deal more effort than is usual. Or, if you have been running a deficit and therefore appear financially weak and generally badly managed, show how this year you will break even and next year you will even move into surplus. You could explain, for example, that the deficit was a necessary outcome of important structural changes and that the organisation is now much stronger and how the project you are writing about is central to the organisation's ongoing development and financial viability.

Sometimes, you may have to delay your application until you have resolved some of your problems. Or at least you may need to bring them to the attention of your management committee and get it to sanction a course of action. You can then show the funder how you are already on the road to sorting out the problem.

With BIG you need to be particularly aware of your apparent failure to meet its assessment criteria. For example, BIG takes equal opportunities and user involvement very seriously. If you cannot show user involvement in your work – and especially the project for which you are trying to get money – you will reduce your chances of success. Therefore, you will need to adopt strategies to demonstrate that although historically you have been weak in the area of user involvement, you are now taking the issue very seriously. You can then show how all future projects will match the funder's criteria. At least with BIG you have the assessment stage to make these points. But part of the applications game is pre-guessing where a funder will mark you down, and showing that by the time this new project gets going you will be well on the way to meeting the funder's concerns.

If there are problems – especially when these will be apparent to the funder – explain what they are and show how you are already moving towards a solution. Don't pretend they don't exist.

Success and failure

Nothing succeeds like success. Funders like to back winners, not losers. If you can demonstrate a track record of success, this is likely to improve your fundraising chances.

What do you think are your real successes and achievements over the last two or three years, which could usefully lend credibility to a fundraising application?

● Successes relating to the organisation as a whole?
● Successful projects, successful events, successful work?
● Individual case study examples of success (suitably disguised if confidentiality is required)?
● Success in attracting support or sponsorship?
● Objectives that have been achieved?

Learn from failure

Although everyone wants to be successful, even the best-run organisations fail from time to time. Sometimes the project is experimental and simply does not work. Perhaps circumstances or needs will change. Occasionally a grant will be cut or further funding will fail to materialise. Sometimes it is due to circumstances beyond your control.

Whatever the reasons for failure, be honest. Trumpet your successes by all means, but don't necessarily hide your failures. There may be lessons to be learned, experience to be disseminated and credibility to be won from explaining why the project didn't work out quite as planned.

This chapter has covered the basic ingredients of a good application. Having got this information together, you need to stand back a little and look at your application from a slightly different viewpoint to see if you can make a good application into an even better one. The following chapter tries to shift the emphasis away from the information you need to assemble to the perspective you need to have.

Dealing with weaknesses: an example

You have lost money in each of the last three years. The funder may look at your accounts and think that you are slowly but surely going under and you will not be able to undertake the work you have asked to be funded. Obviously you need to reassure the funder that this isn't the case. How can you do this?

- **Explain why the losses came about**
  For example, are they the result of a major relocation or restructuring (financial or staff)? If so, you can show how you have reached the end of this process and are now moving forward. Or are they the result of losing a major grant or income stream? If so, show what steps you have taken to address the short-term problem of replacing the funding (or making the necessary financial savings) and that you have put or are putting in place a new, secure and more wide-ranging income base.

- **Show how you are progressing well this year**
  Hopefully this year things are going better. Can you show that you have budgeted for a financial surplus and that you are on target to meet this? This implies that things genuinely have begun to turn around.

- **Use a business plan**
  Draw up a business plan (if you haven't done so already) which shows how you expect to make a regular surplus over the next three to five years, again pointing out the significant changes you have made and will be making to enable you to achieve this.

- **Indicate the funder's role in your development**
  It may be that you are applying to the funder specifically to help you get out of your current financial mess. Again, you will need to give the funder the confidence that you have thought through your long-term income and expenditure requirements and that you have a workable strategy in place to achieve this. Then show the funder the importance of your work and how they can be a key investor in your organisation's future growth and development.

Make a list of some of your weak points and how you might respond

Weakness	Explanation

4

Improving your chances

Having got together all the basic ingredients, you now need to stand back a little and bring some new thinking to bear on the applications process. This should enable you to present your work in a way that grabs the donor's attention and helps your application stand out from the crowd.

Think in project terms

The whole purpose of fundraising is to get hold of enough money to meet the day-to-day running costs for your organisation and its work and any capital expenditure that your organisation is incurring, plus the resources you need for your future development.

But it is far easier to raise money for something specific than for the organisation as a whole. This is because donors can then match the support they give to a specific piece of work or expenditure, to a particular activity or outcome. They will feel that their money is doing something specific.

So, rather than asking for a generous contribution to your organisation or towards its overall financial needs, it is far better to ask for support for a particular aspect of your work or to pay for a specific item of expenditure.

Thinking of your work in project terms and designing projects that will attract support is a key factor of successful fundraising and proposal writing. However, you need to consider that, for a project to run, more than just the direct costs of the project are required.

Full project costs

All organisations have central or core costs, such as management, research and development and financial planning, which are essential to keeping the organisation going. However, they may not be attractive to donors, many of which state that they prefer to or will only fund projects.

The whole core costs/project funding debate has moved on significantly over the last few years, following work by ACEVO (Association of Chief Executives of Voluntary Organisations) and other organisations. What they were saying several years ago is now accepted by many of the larger funders.

To quote from the ACEVO website:

> Historically, third sector organisations have struggled to secure funding for their overhead costs, leading to underinvestment in management and leadership, internal and external infrastructure, strategic development and governance. This difficulty has been exacerbated by a trend on the part of the sector's funders towards funding the direct costs of projects rather than overheads or 'core funding'. Failure to secure funding for overhead costs makes important services, including public services, and the organisations that deliver them, unsustainable. Both government and the sector's representatives have agreed on a solution: full cost recovery (FCR).
>
> Under FCR, organisations and their funders ensure that the price of contracts and grants reflects the full costs of delivery, including the legitimate portion of overhead costs. This commitment poses challenges for both organisations and their funders.
>
> - Third sector organisations must cost their projects and services on an accurate, defensible and sustainable basis.
> - Government must ensure that all public bodies fund services sustainably, by permitting the inclusion in prices of the relevant portion of overheads, and ensure that prices are determined on a realistic basis.

HM Treasury first endorsed the principle of full cost recovery in its 2002 cross-cutting review, *The Role of the Voluntary Sector in Service Delivery*. The review stated that 'Funders should recognise that it is legitimate for providers to include the relevant element of overheads in their cost estimates for providing a given service under service agreement or contract'.

The review stated that the deadline for statutory funders to implement full cost recovery was April 2006.

All departments will incorporate the review's funding recommendations fully into their procurement policies by ensuring that the price for contracts reflects the full cost of the service, including the legitimate portion of overhead costs by April 2006.

Leaving aside the ongoing debate about the extent to which FCR has been implemented, particularly by government departments and local authorities, your organisation will probably approach funders that use the FCR model, as well as others who are open to the arguments that it is a better way to fund.

There's no such thing as core funding!

Charities often say they can get funding for projects or for capital spending but not for their administrative or core costs.

To tackle this, the first step is to eliminate these core costs as a separate item from your thinking. You do not have any costs other than those necessary for carrying out your work or projects. If you do you are breaking the law, because a charity can only spend money wholly and exclusively on its charitable purposes.

So, you need to:

- think of your work as a series of projects
- build your full overhead costs into each of these activities (full cost recovery)
- recognise that if the overhead costs have not been paid for, then the project is not being fully funded.

For more information on how to do this, see chapter 5.

Early work by ACEVO proposed three strategies that funders might adopt in their grantmaking. These were described as 'alternative models of funding that seek to break the mould of the debate about core and project funding' and can be summarised as:

- **full project funding** in which all reasonable associated costs are met as part of a funding package – this is referred to as 'the business model'
- **development funding** through which the internal infrastructure costs of an organisation are met for a time to enable it to grow and develop
- **strategic funding** through which the funder recognises the need for an organisation to exist – to meet its own objectives – and is prepared to contribute over an agreed period.

The first of these has attracted most ongoing interest and development, but there are and will continue to be funders that will give support for the core costs of your work, either through development or strategic funding.

Some of these forms of funding will be appropriate for some types of funder, for some types of voluntary organisation, and at particular stages of a voluntary organisation's life. Funders are likely to use a combination of these strategies, and for some only one or two of the strategies will seem suitable.

Full cost recovery means recovering or funding the full costs of a project or service. In addition to the costs directly associated with the project, such as staff and equipment, projects will also draw on the rest of the organisation. For example, adequate finance, human resources, management and IT systems, are also integral components of any project or service.

The full cost of any project therefore includes an element of each type of overhead cost, which should be allocated on a comprehensive, robust and defensible basis.

ACEVO highlights the following benefits of full cost recovery for your organisation and for funders.

Benefits of full cost recovery for your organisation

All organisations have overhead costs, associated with:

- management and leadership
- infrastructure and accommodation

43

- finance, governance and controls, and
- strategic development.

These overhead costs must be met in order for the organisation to survive, grow and develop. They are therefore essential to all its outputs. Under full cost recovery, organisations analyse their overhead costs and allocate them across the outputs, projects and services they deliver. Under this system the cost of each output includes an appropriate element of funding for overhead costs.

By implementing full cost recovery, third sector organisations develop a full understanding of the true cost of their work. Such an understanding is essential for effective financial management and strategic planning across any organisation.

Understanding the true cost of your work will enable you to have a more informed dialogue with funders in:

- grant-seeking
- competitive tendering
- fundraising.

Full cost recovery will help organisations avoid the problems involved in:

- **generating shortfalls** in funding through the use of arbitrary per-centages for management costs
- **cost conversion**: attempting to repackage overhead costs as projects
- **cost donation**: attempting to find scarce 'core funding' to cover your overhead costs.

Full cost recovery is standard practice across the commercial sector, and is rapidly becoming standard practice in the third sector.

Working to the full cost recovery model, you need to be clear what the advantages are for the funder as well as your organisation. In some cases you may find yourself having to convince the funder this the best way for them to fund.

Benefits of full cost recovery for funders

- **Accuracy:** full cost recovery gives funders a true reflection of the cost of the projects and services they support.
- **Transparency:** full cost recovery provides the only clear and defensible cost allocation method, promoting trust between funders and the organisations they fund.
- **Efficiency:** full cost recovery reduces the time spent repackaging and analysing costs by funders and funded organisations.
- **Appropriateness:** full cost recovery ensures that funders pay for all and only the overheads that support *their* project, rather than subsidising other projects.
- **Sustainability:** only under full cost recovery can funded organisations survive in the long term, so that their projects and services continue.

Failure to recover full costs can mean that TSOs [third sector organisations] have to divert funding intended for service provision into paying overheads, or subsidise service provision from other sources such as donor income. Ultimately, failure to cover overheads may lead to organisations shrinking or collapsing.

(*Working with the Third Sector*, National Audit Office, 2005)

As a result, government at all levels – in theory at least – should recognise the three funding definitions. Many major grant-making trusts and BIG already work to the full cost recovery model. Therefore, it is now almost always worth framing your funding application around the ACEVO definitions. You can start your application by saying: 'I am writing to ask for full project funding for . . .' or 'I am writing to ask for development funding for . . .' or whatever. All major funders will now recognise this new code and accept that you are putting the legitimate management and other overhead costs into the project budget (for more detail see chapter 5).

But what about getting funding for the boring bits . . .?

ACEVO's work has definitely made project fundraising that much easier. However, it immediately raises the question of how you get support for those parts of your work that are less attractive to donors. There are a number of possible ways of overcoming this problem.

- Cost all your projects realistically. Include all the items of expenditure you are likely to incur. This is dealt with further in chapter 5.
- Include an allocation of overhead costs in your project budget (full cost recovery). It is reasonable that every project should make an

appropriate contribution to the general costs of running the organ-isation. This allocation should be made on some suitable basis that you are prepared to justify, rather than a figure plucked out of the air (see chapter 5).

- Be creative in how you match your income to your expenditure. Be realistic in how you cost your projects. Be imaginative in designing attractive projects to raise money for.
- Use your core grants and general fundraising income to pay for the administration costs or the parts of your work for which it is especially difficult to raise money.

The problem can arise that your fundraising for one particular project is so successful that you have raised more than you need or can reasonably spend on the work. What do you then do?

You must do something. If you have asked for money for a particular purpose, then you are obliged to spend it for that purpose. You will have to go back to at least some of your supporters and ask if you can use their money to extend the project or spend their grant on another related piece of work. They will almost certainly agree to this. Or you might decide to expand the project or allocate any surplus to next year's budget; again, you should keep your supporters informed.

Difficulties arise when fundraising threatens to determine the work of the organisation. Many organisations find that it is easy to raise money for a particular purpose or decide to approach a particular line of funding which is only available for a very particular purpose, and then reorganise themselves to fit in with this. Ideally, you should first decide what you want to do and then raise money for that. There will inevitably be some trade-off between what you can easily raise money for and what you want to do, but you should try to keep the two in a reasonable balance. Otherwise the organisation will lose purpose and direction.

Where you judge the project to be unattractive for fundraising, you will need to think carefully. It will be a waste of your time to seek funds for something that is unlikely to appeal to donors. In such circumstances, you might:

- find a way of restructuring the project or presenting it in a different way so that it appears more attractive to donors
- think of something else to raise money for, which will be more attrac-tive. Most organisations can juggle their budgets so that the more

attractive projects are put forward for fundraising and the remainder of the money comes through their general fundraising income

- discuss whether there are alternative ways of financing the project (for example through charging fees for services or developing a new income stream). Many people tend to be rather grants-obsessed. Always ask yourself whether short-term grants are the only way or the best way of resourcing the project.

A fundable project should be:

- **specific** – an identifiable item of expenditure or aspect of the organisation's work
- **important** – both to the organisation and to the cause or need it is meeting. If there is some long-term impact, that will be an added bonus
- **effective** – there should be a clear and positive outcome
- **realistic** – the work proposed should be achievable
- **good value** – the work should be a good use of the donor's money
- **topical** – the project should be looking at current issues and concerns
- **relevant** – it should be relevant to the donor and the donor's particular funding concerns
- **bite-sized** – it should not be too large or too small for a donor to support, although the cost might be shared through several smaller grants. If it is too large, it might be broken down further into sub-projects.

Making a project more fundable

Once you have decided that you are going to raise money for a project, the next step is to see whether and how you can make it more attractive to donors. Donors will certainly want to see value for their money, and possibly some long-term impact on the organisation in which they are investing. This improvement process will also allow you to think through what you are doing, and may help you create a better project – which is an added benefit.

EXERCISE

Go round the organisation and get a list of 20 things that colleagues want funded. Rank them in terms of fundability. Do they form the basis of a good fundraising programme?

Grant-winning ideas and fundable projects

What is a good idea? A good idea is something that will have immediate appeal with donors as being different, lively, worthwhile and therefore worth funding. The donor's first response is more likely to be 'Gosh, that sounds good; we ought to be backing that', rather than, 'I've had 10 applications like that in the last month, and none of them are likely to achieve very much'.

Good ideas are central to good fundraising. Even the very best application may not make up for a poorly-thought-out project or for something that simply is not very interesting. However, it is difficult to define what constitutes a good idea. Usually it is something that leaps out at you from the page and seems obvious once someone has thought of it. The following are some ingredients of a good idea.

- It meets a **really important and urgent need**.
- It is **fresh or interesting** (or at least sounds it) and captures the imagination.
- It is – or sounds – **startlingly obvious**, even though nobody has thought of it before.
- It has a **catchy title**.
- It is or appears **innovative**.
- It is **topical** – it fits within current fashions, thinking, concerns.
- It addresses issues of **disadvantage**, a key concern for most funders.
- It is **different** – it stands out in the crowd of more ordinary applications.
- It has **different aspects** which appeal to different funding constituencies (wide appeal).
- It shows value **for money** or **leverage** (a small input with lots of output).
- It **complements and supplements existing provision** or involves collaboration with other agencies.
- It has a **clear and attainable objective**.
- It has **measurable benefits** and specific outputs.
- It is **realistic** and **achievable**.
- It is **fundable** and may even **develop its own income** in the long term.

Evaluating your project

Increasingly funders require the organisations they support to produce some sort of evaluation of the outcome of their work. This can range from a brief statement about what has been achieved with the grant to a more detailed report showing how your project has achieved its objective(s) and to what extent. To do this you need to have measurable objectives for your project and measure the results you achieve.

Many organisations make over-optimistic or even outrageous claims for the outcomes and impact of their work, so take care to be seen to be reasonable. A good evaluation also has the following benefits:

- it brings you credibility with funders
- it suggests ways in which you can improve what you do
- it can suggest a next stage for the further development of the project.

When you design your project you can build in simple ways of getting feedback, which will provide information for evaluating the project later on and perhaps save costs if it is built in at the outset.

Many applications are disappointingly vague about what they will actually do and how they will measure progress. The key things are, firstly, to set some measurable targets (or milestones) and, secondly, to show how discussions about progress will be fed into the management of the project (and, indeed, the management of the organisation). There is little point in saying: 'We are behind (or ahead) of our targets' and then do nothing about it. Monitoring and evaluation is about action and decision-making. You need to show who will take action and when.

This will not only demonstrate how effective you are – and if you can do this you will find it that much easier to obtain funding in the future – but it will also provide you with a tool to manage your project, to make the appropriate changes and adjustments as the work proceeds.

Evaluation can be expensive (for example, professional consultancy, surveys and other market research, or the work involved in the measurement of outcomes). From time to time, it may be appropriate for an organisation to undertake a serious evaluation with the aim of setting the stage for its future development. Indeed the costs of this can be packaged up into a 'project' and be the subject of a fundraising application. But evaluation need not cost much if it is thought through and built into the way the project is run right from the start. It is important that evaluation is independent, and it is vital that you have a credible person or organisation carrying it out. Evaluation of what you do shows a professional approach and, in a competitive world, this can only be an advantage.

Measuring progress

Not all funders require the same information. You need to be clear about what a particular funder requires and make sure you have everything in place at the start of your project to fulfil the funder's monitoring require- ments. You may even decide that the monitoring work involved for some funding streams may be too time-consuming and too much effort for the scale of support.

Some funders will want to receive reports on the progress of your activities. They want to know that their money is being used to set up and run the activities you said it would. This may involve setting targets or milestones for your activities (inputs) and for the services you provide (outputs). This will involve drawing up a plan with dates and key tasks and outputs.

Example of targets for activities and services

The following could be initial milestones or targets for a project working with young people in a rural area.

Activities

Project coordinator appointed	31 January
Publicity distributed	31 March
Minibus obtained	30 April
Services started	1 July

Services

Discussion meetings held with young people in 12 villages by 30 April

10 volunteer leaders trained by 31 May
25 young people regularly attending youth club by 31 December
12 activity days held by 31 December

Measuring your activities and services will show that the project is up and running, but you will also need to demonstrate that you are making progress towards your outcomes. For example, BIG asks award recipients to set milestones for each of the intended outcomes and report on them. This has to be done as part of the application process.

In assessing applications to Reaching Communities, BIG assessors consider the following questions:

- Are there clear milestones and does the applicant have extensive plans to monitor progress in achieving the proposed project outcomes?
- Are there comprehensive, appropriate and inclusive plans in place for measuring and evaluating the success of the project (and for existing projects, has the applicant demonstrated the successes and achievements to date)?

Making your project outcomes SMART

Clearly defining the outcomes of your work is essential to obtaining the funding you need. To be able to carry out effective evaluation of the project these outcomes should be measurable in some way. Some statutory funders, BIG and other funders are increasingly encouraging organisations to set SMART outcomes.

However, there seem to be some differences between funders as to what SMART actually stands for, the main difference being whether the R stands for 'realistic' or 'relevant'.

Specific – your outcomes need to be tightly defined and relate directly to the need you have identified and which you are addressing.

Measurable – you need to be able to measure the change or improvement that your work brings about. You need to record information at the start, during and at the end of the project.

Achievable – refers to the internal capacity of the organisation – the human, material and financial resources available to make the project happen.

Realistic – capable of being achieved with the available resources and within the agreed timescale.

Relevant – have a strong connection to the funder's priorities and activities.

Time-bound – set within specific time periods.

Setting SMART outcomes will enable you to plan your project further and explain to funders just how much you think you will be able to achieve, the scale of change and for how many people over what period. So your outcomes will need to include information such as dates and numbers, not just who and what.

Once you have established your outcomes you need to determine what information will show that these outcomes are being achieved. These further milestones/targets are often called 'outcome indicators' and you need to have some way of measuring them.

Ideally, outcomes will be quantifiable, where you can count the number of things that happen, such as the number of young people actively involved in running the project. However, many outcomes are qualitative and cannot be assessed as easily. This can involve assessing people's views and experiences, such as how isolated young people feel.

The important thing is to be clear what your outcomes are and how you will know that you have (or haven't) achieved them. The funder wants to know that it is making a difference.

It is beyond the scope of this guide to detail how outcomes and indicators can be measured. Helpful resources are available from a number of organisations such as Charities Evaluation Services and the National Association for Voluntary and Community Action (NAVCA). BIG has produced a helpful factsheet for using the outcomes approach which is available at: www.biglotteryfund.org.uk – just type 'outcomes' in the search field.

How to develop good ideas

Respond to new needs as they emerge. You are at the frontline of social provision. The needs you identify today will be met by the established services of tomorrow.

Two heads are better than one. Get together with colleagues to bounce ideas around. Start with your current work, your current projects. What are the next steps? How could things be done differently or better? What new needs are emerging from what you are doing and what can you do about them?

Ask your current, previous and potential users. What do they think about the situation now and in the future? What would they do in your position?

Talk to people, visit other projects; get out and about more. Be inspired by what others are doing and use this to do something inspirational.

Also, keep an eye on the 'marketplace' – see what others are doing. Get hold of other organisations' annual reports. Look at the emerging social business sector. Keep in touch with social trends, emerging fashions and fads.

Write down ideas as soon as you have thought of them, however half-baked or ill-thought-out they appear. If you don't, you'll forget them; if you do, you can develop and refine them over time.

Bring in outsiders who have no preconceptions. This can provide a degree of 'lateral thinking', which will be useful. You know how the buses or the health service should be run, so it is a good bet that outsiders can teach you a thing or two. Stop thinking about what you can't do and about all the problems and difficulties. Develop a positive can-do attitude to your work and your organisation.

Go back to basics. Forget what you are doing now. What might you be doing in an ideal world to deal with the problem or need? Look at your organisation's objects or purposes as enshrined in the founding documents and think about what you would do if you were starting from scratch.

Somewhere, there is an idea that is just right for your organisation, for which it will be easy to raise money, that will enhance your credibility and public image, and which (hopefully) will solve all your financial problems . . . forever.

Adding value

Wherever possible, try to show funders that you are giving and getting maximum value from their support. Investment, leverage and dissemination are all useful concepts in this process.

Investment

An investment (or 'development' expenditure in ACEVO terms) is an expenditure that builds the potential of the organisation and helps it move towards a more successful future. It aims to build a more secure and successful organisation later on rather than simply provide a service now.

It can be an extremely important and cost-effective way of providing support. Some possibilities are listed below.

- **Investing in capacity**: to enable you to undertake more work more effectively or to earn more money from the services you provide.
- **Investing in technology**: to open up new, quicker, lower-cost ways of providing services or to help you move from being a local to a national or international information provider.
- **Investing in efficiency**: to streamline the organisation and cut waste.
- **Investing in training and skills**: to improve the quality and effectiveness of your work.
- **Investing in plant or equipment**: for example, buying a piece of equipment to improve your efficiency or effectiveness.
- **Investing in fundraising**: for example, developing a supporter group which, over time, will generate an increased income.
- **Investing in long-term stability**: for example, generating the resources or information that will enable you to negotiate contracts and service agreements which will underpin your future financial security.

All or any of these can be the subject of a fundraising application. Indeed, you can often put on a gloss that makes the idea appear more planned and better thought out than it in fact was. If you realise that you are currently short of money and have ideas for future income generation, you could dress this up as a stage one/stage two proposal. This is where you show how you have reached the end of the first stage of your development and you need to get to the next stage; you ask for funding to help you get from where you are to where you need to be.

Leverage

Leverage is the process whereby a small amount of support helps create a large amount of impact. This is the ideal position for a donor, so showing leverage can improve your chances of success. There are many ways in which this can be done.

- **Matching grants**: where one donor has promised to pay half the costs if you can raise the rest. Every pound you now raise will release an additional pound of the donor's money. Companies often use this when they match their employees' fundraising activities pound for pound.
- **Challenge grants**: where you ask a donor to promise a certain sum on the condition that you raise the rest by a particular date. This gives the

donor the assurance that their promise of money is being used to lever other sums and the confidence that if you fail to raise the outstanding amounts the original donor owes nothing.

- **Fundraising leverage**: where the support given will enable you to raise a much larger sum. A prize offered for a raffle, for example, may enable you to raise a considerable sum through selling raffle tickets. Or integrated software would allow you to develop a membership and alumni programme worth X hundred thousand pounds a year.
- **Lasting benefit**: your work can have a long-term benefit in the lives of individuals and their communities, and this can last way beyond the time you are supporting them.
- **Use of volunteers**: the value of the work done can be much greater if volunteers rather than paid staff are used.
- **Discounts**: obtaining discounts on purchases or even getting items in your budget donated shows an effective organisation and allows the donor's contribution to go that much further.
- **Problem solving**: by meeting the need now you then save money which would otherwise have to be spent dealing with the consequences (for example, if you stop young people turning to crime).

Dissemination

People will be interested in the impact of your work and its effect on alleviating the problem. If the money is for undertaking research or producing a publication, they will want to be told how the research findings will be disseminated or how the publication will be distributed. If the money is for some form of innovation or a pilot project, they will want to be shown how the success of the project will be measured and what will be done subsequently to promote the lessons learned and encourage others to replicate the ideas. Dissemination should be properly costed and included in your budget.

Dissemination can be linked to the concept of leverage. For example, a locally run project can be copied throughout the country if it can be shown to be effective, so X thousand pounds given to you to test out the idea means that ultimately the whole country might benefit.

The application for funds is just the first part of the process. Obtaining the money and undertaking the work outlined in the proposal is the second stage. The third stage is to make use of the outcome in some way: where this is an important ingredient of the proposal, it should be fully discussed in the application.

5

Costing a project

The budget

The budget is a central element of your application. It sets out your financial need and provides the base around which your argument for support is developed.

People are often frightened by the budgeting process. They give it an aura and mystique that it simply does not have, and wrongly assume that it is a skill possessed by only the privileged few. Budgeting is no more than a careful costing of all the items of expenditure involved in the work you are proposing. But since many of the items cannot be precisely determined or allocated, there is plenty of scope for creativity in coming to a final figure for your fundraising.

A common mistake is for people to under-cost their budgets. Perhaps they feel that if they apply for less, they stand a better chance of getting the money. But if you always apply for too little, you will end up in a financial mess.

It is better to go for a larger sum when raising money, particularly where the project is well-thought-through and likely to be attractive to donors. You will then be concentrating your effort on the fundraising that is most likely to succeed. By including overhead costs (see page 61) and allowing for other costs that you might have otherwise omitted (full cost recovery), you will be bringing money into your organisation that you would otherwise have to raise in other ways.

The trick is to demonstrate the benefits of the project and how much will be achieved by the work rather than showing how little it will cost to do it.

Remember, fundraising is about change rather than money. Sell the idea of change, and then tell the donor how much it will cost.

The budgeting process

There are basically six stages in the budgeting process. Here are two examples of projects, one mainly capital, the second mainly revenue and incorporating the full cost recovery method (see page 41 and onwards). They follow the same six stages.

Stages in the budgeting process

1   Describe the project
2   Write down the expenditure needs
3   Cost each item as carefully as you can
4   Add up all the costs
5   Examine the total and amend the budget if necessary
6   Agree the budget

Example 1 – Upgrading a community centre

Stage 1
Describe in detail the scope of the project and what you intend to do with the money. Compare the following statements:

- We plan to refurbish our community centre.
- We plan to develop our community centre by creating new community initiatives and increasing capacity.

These are two very different fundraising propositions. The first is internally focused and centres on maintenance. The second is about using a building to advance the organisation and its work. It involves additional costs and so will be more expensive, but it is also likely to be more attractive to donors. In ACEVO terms it would be called 'development funding' (see page 42).

This applies to any kind of capital or equipment purchase. 'We want to buy a building' or 'We need a minibus' are pretty dull statements. 'We want to release the creative talents of our young people by setting up a community arts centre', or 'We want to overcome the problems of rural isolation by bringing older people together twice a week' are much more engaging. It's not about your needs: it's about your users' needs. Talk about them, not you.

Stage 2

Write a list of all the budget heads of expenditure. Then consider whether you have left anything out. Refurbishing the community centre could include:

- feasibility studies
- architect
- quantity surveyor/structural engineer (if there is major building work)
- health and safety advice
- construction costs
- furniture and fittings
- security (system and people)
- decoration
- equipment
- maintenance
- sundry and contingency costs.

Stage 3

Cost each item using the best estimates you can.

- **Professional fees** (for example, an architect): get different quotes and see what is included in each. Can you get drawings and plans done for free on a joint risk venture (i.e. if you get the money the architect gets the contract, but if you don't raise the money you don't owe the architect anything)?
- **Furniture and fittings**: you may be able to get some of these items donated (for example paint, chairs and settees) or at least at a discount. If so, quote prices before discount and treat any discount as in-kind support and part of your fundraising.
- **Security**: this can include people as well as equipment. For example, if you are open in the evening you may need extra security such as CCTV and additional reception cover. You need to take account of any increased running costs in your budget for running the centre.
- **Maintenance**: buildings get bashed about; there is wear and tear on equipment. Broken equipment will need to be replaced and the place kept in good order. You may even need to appoint a warden or caretaker

for the first time. All these are extra running costs, which you will need to take into account.

Stage 4

Add up the estimated costs to create a total budget for the project. Some of these costs will be one-off (such as construction costs); others will be ongoing (such as repair, maintenance and caretaking).

The one-off costs tend to be fairly straightforward, but make sure you get more than one quote. The ongoing costs can be more problematic as the budget for refurbishment will not usually cover these. But you could think of including additional first year running costs in your fundraising budget, to help you get going in your new premises. Add in lost income for the time the existing centre will be closed for refurbishment. The basic rule is: decide what you think is reasonable and, at this stage, put down your best estimate of the cost.

Stage 5

Examine the total to decide whether it provides a reasonable basis for your fundraising. Is the end figure you have arrived at too high, too low or about right? This decision is more likely to be based on the overall costs set against the benefits you will be aiming to deliver for your community. For example, £100,000 for a thriving centre that will be used by 750 people a week is not much money; £30,000 so that a couple of small youth groups can meet on a Wednesday and Thursday evening sounds a lot. Further, if you can show that once all this work is done you will then have a sustainable income base from the hire-out charges you will be able to levy, this makes it doubly attractive to a funder. Attach a three-year plan to demonstrate all of this.

It is usually possible to re-cost the project so that the total comes out significantly higher or lower. Many of the items are simply best guesses at this stage, and only time will tell.

Once you are confident that your estimated costs are all plausible – that is, you can defend them when they are put under the spotlight by a sceptical grants assessor – and that the project represents real value for money, the final question is whether the total required is too much for one donor to support. If so, approach several. You can even break down the project into bite-sized chunks, asking one donor to support the children's playroom, another the computers for the homework club and IT centre, etc.

Stage 6
You now have a final, agreed budget for your project. This is the target for your fundraising, and the basis on which you can create a fundraising plan.

Example 2 – An outreach project

When obtaining funding for a project, you need to address the issue of the overhead or core costs necessary for the project to run. It is not simply a question of calculating the direct costs. Charities often say that they can get funding for a project or for capital spending, but not for their administrative or core costs. The key to overcoming this is to eliminate these core costs as a separate item in your thinking. You do not have any core costs. The only costs you carry are those necessary for undertaking your work, unless you have people who are doing absolutely nothing. Therefore, you need to build these overhead costs into all your activities and recognise that, unless they have been funded, insufficient money has been raised for the project.

You will want to include an allocation of overheads or a contribution to your organisation's central administration costs, especially when applying for salaries and other revenue funding. Termed full cost recovery, this is increasingly expected by major funders.

The basis on which these costs are apportioned will vary from project to project, but it should be based on a sensible apportionment of the costs. The budgeting is the same six-stage process. To avoid repetition, we are only expanding on points that are particularly relevant to revenue applications – otherwise the points made in the previous example above are all valid.

Stage 1 – Describe the project
We wish to help people out of poverty and to take more control over their lives by helping them achieve greater financial independence. We will do this by establishing a new money advice service.

Stage 2 – Write down the expenditure
This will include the direct costs of the project:

● salary/national insurance for the money advice worker
● basic equipment needs (new desk, computer, etc.)
● post, telephone, stationery, etc.

- volunteer expenses
- travel

and the overheads allocated to the project:

- premises costs (rent, rates, heat, light, cleaning, etc.)
- central costs (insurance, bank charges, accountancy, audit, etc.)
- management/supervision costs
- clerical support.

There's no such thing as 'core costs'. All your costs are spent on the work you do. Therefore make sure you build all relevant overhead costs into each project application you make, and call it 'full project funding'.

Putting down all the direct costs is usually a fairly straightforward process. The difficult part can be remembering all those hidden costs which are vital to the project's success but which are far less obvious (for example, occupancy of the building, management and administration costs). However, make sure you get all of them down.

ACEVO has developed a *Full Cost Recovery Toolkit*, which is available as a free download (www.fullcostrecovery.org.uk). It uses a simple six-stage process to help organisations calculate and understand the total cost of each activity, including an appropriate portion of overhead costs. This involves calculating the total overhead costs of your organisation and then allocating costs across your different projects. At the end of the process all your overhead costs are allocated to projects, giving you the full cost needed to run each project or activity.

Typical overheads:

- salaries of core staff such as managers, administrators, finance staff, cleaners and caretakers
- salaries of staff, including managers working on this project and a number of other projects
- meetings of the trustees or management committee and their expenses
- audit, accountancy and legal fees associated with running your whole organisation
- rent, heating, lighting, maintenance and insurance for premises your project shares with other projects

- administration and office costs that support several projects includ-ing your project. For example: stationery, phone bills, postage, photocopying and computers
- professional fees associated with strategic planning
- fundraising for the costs of supporting the organisation as a whole
- training of support staff and senior staff
- networking and attendance at conferences or partnership work that benefits the project you want us to fund.

(from BIG Lottery Fund's 'Applying for your project overheads' – available to download from www.biglotteryfund.org.uk)

Stage 3 – Cost each item

Again, the direct costs are fairly easy to put a figure on. You know the expected salary of the worker. You know what kind of basic equipment he or she will need. However, how do you calculate the central costs?

The most usual way is to look at the percentage of space the person will take up and the proportion of office facilities he or she will share. For example, if the outreach worker will use one-fifth of the office building, allocate one-fifth of the premises costs (rent, rates, heat, light, etc.) to the project. If the outreach worker shares office facilities equally with eight other full-time workers, allocate one-ninth of the post, telephone, stationery and other such bills. If the outreach project occupies a quarter of the manager's time in terms of development, support and supervision, allocate a quarter of the manager's salary and national insurance to the project.

Make a reasonable estimate. In the end, all you are trying to achieve is a realistic figure for the cost to the organisation as a whole of running this new project. It is not a fiddle. You are not trying quietly to bump up the figures and apply for more than you should. Rather, you are simply aiming to avoid the position whereby you suddenly find the telephone bill has risen substantially on account of this new project and this becomes a drain on your resources.

Stage 4 – Total the costs

Total the costs on the above basis. Make sure that you explain how you have arrived at the costs in notes to your budget, for example:

Salary and national insurance	£21,000
Premises costs[1]	£8,200
Supervision and support [2]	£9,000
Volunteer expenses [3]	£7,200
Other	£7,600
TOTAL	£53,000

Notes

1 equal to 20% of occupancy costs
2 equal to 25% of management and 12.5% of admin salaries
3 calculated on the basis of six full-time equivalent volunteers at £800 per annum travel costs and £400 training costs

Stage 5

When looking at the overall costs again, you can make changes if you are not happy with them. Reassess the resources required and adjust the percentages you have used accordingly. Remember that you may be asked to justify the basis of your calculation, so it has to appear reasonable.

If you already have a grant that covers some or all of your central costs (say from your local authority), you can use this to show that you have already covered some of the costs of the project. For example, if you can show that you have raised £17,200, you have already covered your premises and supervision costs from another grant. It is important that you do this for four reasons:

1 It demonstrates to the funder that you have not forgotten anything. If you simply leave these costs out because they have already been paid for, then the funder may get the impression that you haven't thought the project through properly.
2 The hardest part of your fundraising is getting the fundraising ball rolling. Once you have started getting money in, other funders take confidence from this and pledge their support accordingly. So if you can show that some of the required money is already there, this gives the whole process an impetus that it otherwise would not have.
3 It shows that you have a really good grasp of finance, knowing what parts of your work are already covered by existing grants and income, and which are not.

4   It creates extra leverage to your application because the new funder only
has to give two-thirds of the total to make this wonderful work happen.

Stage 6 – Agree the budget
As with the example of the community centre (see page 57), you should
now be clear where the money for the different parts of the organisation's
costs are coming from, as well as having an agreed fundraising plan.
Project fundraising can feel a bit like juggling – keeping lots of different
fundraising balls in the air at the same time. The advantage is that if you
can do it, you broaden your fundraising scope and become less dependent
on one major funder.

Common mistakes in budgeting

Forgotten costs

Have you included all the items you will be spending money on? What
about training and attending courses? Buying necessary publications?
Travel and subsistence? Pension contributions as well as national
insurance? Who is going to pay for these if you don't raise the money? Or
will this extra expenditure just increase your deficit?

Hidden costs

Every project consumes office space, heating, lighting, telephone, postage,
the cost of supervision by the director and the management committee.
You need to include a reasonable element of them in your budget for the
project. Since it is far easier to raise money for projects than it is for administration or running the office, by allocating your overhead costs onto your
projects, you will use the glamour of the project to get the unattractive
administrative costs paid for.

Understated costs

It is easy to put too low a cost in your budget. There are several reasons for
this. There is a tendency to underestimate the costs of the project because
you think that the fundraising will be difficult. Or you may be basing your
estimate on this year's costs, or worse, on last year's, but your budget is for
next year when inflation will have increased the cost of everything. Get as
good an estimate as possible for the cost of each item and allow something
for inflation.

When you are applying for a grant over several years, allow for inflation on an estimated basis for the second and subsequent years (you would normally state the assumptions you have made in a footnote to the budget).

If you leave out any item of expenditure from your budget or put in a cost which is less than what will actually be incurred, then you will be out of pocket. If you consistently do this, then you will have a financial problem. It also looks extremely bad from a fundraising point of view if you have to go back to a funder asking for more money simply because you underestimated the costs.

Not doing what you say you'll do

If you say that you will do something, and you take money on that basis, then you must spend the money in the way you have proposed. If you can't, then you will have to discuss the situation with the donor, or return the money. Therefore, don't promise what you cannot deliver simply because it would make the proposal more attractive to the funder.

Some donors may require you to spend the grant precisely as you have indicated in your budget, and require audited accounts demonstrating that you have done just this. Other donors are happy so long as you have spent the money roughly as detailed in the budget for the purposes set out in the application (they do not care if you have spent more on some items, less on others; they are more interested in the fact that the work you have proposed has actually been done).

Funding regimes are generally getting tighter rather than looser. If you have any concerns about the terms of a grant, or are expecting that there may be changes for whatever good reason, contact the donor sooner rather than later and explain the situation. Donors appreciate openness and are generally happy to be flexible in these kinds of circumstances. However, they get annoyed if they think you have tried to go behind their backs or have misapplied money. In any case, your auditor will want to examine the basis on which the grants were received and how the money was spent. You may want to check with the donor at the time you accept the grant what reporting arrangements (if any) will be required.

Improving your communication skills

Writing in plain English

Faced with the task of writing an application, some people find it hard to put their thoughts together in a clear, logical way. Others develop a writer's block, so that although they have thought through what they want to say, they don't actually get round to putting anything in writing.

An application is no more than answering simple questions such as:

● Who are you?
● What do you currently do?
● What do you want to do?
● Why is this work important?
● What do you need to enable you to do it?
● How can the donor help you?

If you were answering these questions in conversation, you would become really enthusiastic. And in doing so, you would then enthuse the person you were approaching for money.

In your written application, you have to try to create the same sense of upbeat enthusiasm as you would in conversation. Picture yourself chatting at a bar or over coffee, trying to persuade someone of the importance of what you are doing and why he or she should support it. That is what your written application is all about.

The following are some other points to bear in mind.

- You should put down your thoughts in an ordered way, and be as clear and succinct as you can.
- You should make every word work for you, as you have limited space and the attention span of the reader may be short.
- Your application is being read along with hundreds of others each month. It should be clearly set out and easy to read.

A well-written application can make all the difference

A well-written application will certainly improve your chances of success. You will not only have organised your ideas and the argument for supporting you in a more persuasive and readable way, but you will have given the reader the impression that you are well-organised and capable; sufficiently so to be entrusted with the funder's money, as the following (true) story shows.

A friend (whom we shall call Paul) was raising money for a conference in Manchester in which homeless people would speak out about homelessness issues. He was jointly organising this with Peter, who worked for a homelessness charity. They agreed that they would approach a major company based in the area.

Peter organised a meeting with the company without telling Paul, who was putting together a written application. Peter rang Paul after the meeting to say not to bother submitting an application as the company wasn't interested. Paul said it was too late as he had already posted it. Paul got a phone call the next day to say that the company was giving £1,500 to the conference. This was based purely on the fact that the application accurately reflected both a really exciting project and an understanding of the company's desire to be seen as a good corporate citizen.

Some common writer's diseases

Verbicide

Using words whose meaning has been killed. Avoid using jargon – the words that only you and the professionals in your field understand. In an application you are usually talking to people who know little of the detail of what you are doing, and are unlikely to understand the specialist words which you take for granted.

> We believe that children, given the right environment, have an enormous, but often untapped, potential to learn. The concept of the learning organisation/company, in many ways, has now become commonplace. We believe that this concept, replicated in communities, could have significant benefits.

What is a 'learning organisation' or 'learning company'? Although this is central to the application it is never explained. Therefore, unless the funder is an authority on educational issues they will not understand what the project is really about.

> Short-term respite care and flexible day care are the two most valuable forms of support for sufferers of Alzheimer's disease, which allow the carer to cope longer in the community.

What on earth does this mean? What is flexible day care and short-term respite care? And why are they valuable? You may know the answers. Your readers (unless they are specialists in the caring business) are unlikely to.

Verbitis

Using inflamed words, such as unsubstantiated superlatives. Words and phrases such as 'desperate', 'unique', 'a major new initiative' have lost their meaning through overuse and should be avoided if possible. The reader will also be reading dozens of other applications, all of which show desperate needs and unique solutions to the urgent problem. They want to know the facts and the figures, not the generalities expressed in the same meaningless superlatives.

Also, avoid the 'everybody knows' syndrome, where you make a bland statement on the assumption that the reader will understand its full significance.

We all know that crime in general and youth crime in particular is on the increase. We also know that government initiatives to tackle these problems have failed.

Do we? In any case this doesn't convince the reader that you are on top of your subject. If you can't show a deep understanding of the issues, how can you persuade the reader that you have a clearly workable solution?

Our college is a unique institution in British higher education . . . Our facilities are woefully inadequate . . . We operate in a very desolate and most deprived area.

This comes from a major university appeal in London. It raises more questions than answers. Be specific. Explain exactly what you mean. Why is the institution unique? Why are the facilities inadequate? Why is the area desolate? How deprived is it?

Be positive

- So many applications are couched in 'hopes' and 'maybes'. Be upbeat.
  - Don't say 'This project aims to'; say 'We will'.
  - Don't say 'It is our hope that'; say 'We expect to'.
  - Don't say 'If this project didn't happen then'; say 'This project will'.
- So many applications are full of false gloom.
  - Don't say 'If nothing is done the situation will just get worse and worse'; say: 'We can work to ensure that things get much better'.

Verbosity

Waffling on and on. You drown the meaning in a sea of useless words. Make every word work for you. Use a red pen to strike out what is meaningless, what adds nothing to your case. If there is very little left after doing this, then this gives you the opportunity to make a better case.

Within our play centre, staff are required to enable us to register with social services and therefore operate within the law. A particularly high level of skill and understanding is needed in this sensitive area and therefore we feel it particularly useful to have the continuity of qualified staff to maintain the high level of confidence needed in the provision of this service, that is so vital to maintain free access to the centre.

This paragraph is elaborating on the need for paid staff to run a play centre within a community education facility. Apart from the point that paid, skilled staff are required for the play centre, how much of the rest of this paragraph is necessary?

There are two further and extremely common means of padding out applications.

- Many organisations describe their structure along these lines: 'XXX is a registered charity and a voluntary organisation'. This is normally redundant information. Your legal status will be obvious from the nature of your work and your letterhead. A donor will only want to know if you are *not* a charity, as this can affect how the grant is paid over.
- Towards the end of the application, many people sign off with long-winded pleasantries, such as: 'I hope you will be able to give favourable consideration to our request for support and if you would like to discuss this initiative further or require more information, please do not hesitate to contact me at the above address.'

Make yourselves sound more active and dynamic by using the active rather than passive voice.

'We helped Beth to . . .' rather than 'Beth was helped by our organisation to . . .'

'We work closely with . . .' rather than 'A partnership was formed between us and . . .'

Verbification

Producing a continuous stream of syllables where something could be expressed more succinctly simply by tightening up your language.

- Avoid longer words where shorter words will do:
  - not *personal motorised transportation*, but *private car*
  - not *the anticipated cost of the project*, but *the project's budget*
- Avoid long sentences. Use punctuation to make the meaning clearer.
- Avoid long paragraphs, which can become unreadable.
- Aim for a tabloid rather than a broadsheet style.

'There's no way I talk in clichés.'

So avoid them like the plague!

Some practical next steps

- **Buy yourself a red pen**. Use it to shorten and tighten up your next application, a highlighter to note the points that are unclear, badly explained or which need more information, and a pencil to make marginal notes.
- **Find yourself a journalist** – possibly on your local newspaper. Journalists are used to writing for popular consumption and fitting what they want to say into limited space. They may be able to offer you valuable tips and advice on your writing style.
- **Find yourself a fundraising buddy** – someone else who is writing fundraising applications. Agree to read and comment on his or her applications if he or she does the same for yours. The buddy should know little or nothing about your work, because most donors are in the same position. Ask the buddy to tell you which bits he or she doesn't understand, what you have left out and whether you have made a good case.

EXERCISE

Rewrite the following sentences:

- It would be our hope that you might fund this project.
- A demonstrated commitment to cooperation and collaboration forms the cornerstone of this partnership.
- This book was written on the understanding that it would provide . . .
- We can assure you that any contribution you would be able to make would be used to . . .
- Your grant has proved to be of great significance to this organisation, and we would like to express our gratitude.

Or look at the following supplied by the Plain English Campaign:

What on earth do these sentences mean?

1 'Making a skill adjustment.'
2 'Achieving a positive budget variance.'
3 'Meaningful downturn in aggregate output.'
4 'Grain-consuming animal units.'
5 'An unselected roll-back to idle.'
6 'Localised capacity deficiencies.'
7 'High-quality learning environments are a necessary pre-condition for facilitation and enhancement of the ongoing learning process.'
8 'If there are any points on which you require explanation or further particulars we shall be glad to furnish such additional details as may be required by telephone.'
9 'It is important that you shall read the notes, advice and information detailed opposite then complete the form overleaf (all sections) prior to its immediate return to the council by way of the envelope provided.'
10 'Your enquiry about the use of the entrance area at the library for the purpose of displaying posters and leaflets about welfare and supplementary benefit rights, gives rise to the question of the provenance and authoritativeness of the material to be displayed. Posters and leaflets issued by the Central Office of

Information, the Department of Health and Social Security and other authoritative bodies are usually displayed in libraries, but items of a disputatious or polemic kind, whilst not necessarily excluded, are considered individually.'

Answers

1 Making a lot of staff redundant.
2 Making a lot of staff redundant.
3 A recession.
4 Farm animals such as cows, pigs or sheep.
5 The plane's engine failed in mid-flight.
6 Traffic bottlenecks.
7 Children need good schools.
8 Please ring if you have any questions.
9 Please read the notes opposite before you fill in the form. Then send it back to us as soon as possible in the envelope provided.
10 Thank you for your letter asking for permission to put up posters in the library. Before we can give you an answer we will need to see a copy of the posters to make sure they won't offend anyone.

EXERCISE

The cardinal sins of proposal writing are:

1 verbicide
2 verbitis
3 verbosity
4 verbification.

Take a fundraising application you or a colleague have previously written and rewrite it avoiding the four Vs. Aim to cut its length by at least 25%.

Tips for better writing

Do

- write in shorter sentences
- break up longer sentences into a number of sentences
- use bullet points to break up long sections of text
- vary the length of sentences to avoid monotony
- use shorter rather than longer words. Say 'about' rather than 'approximately'; 'try' rather than 'endeavour'; 'often' rather than 'frequently')
- use facts rather than opinions
- keep it short and simple, but make sure you say all you need
- make it clear and logical
- keep cross-references to a minimum, otherwise it can get too confusing
- improve the visual appearance and readability by using shorter paragraphs, headings and sub-heads, tables and bullet points rather than continuous prose
- write for the reader, with an understanding of his or her level of knowledge and perception of the problem.

Eh?

Pseuds Corner in *Private Eye* usually provides an object lesson in how not to write. For example:

> The folk/fairytale Cinderella has a four thousand year old history and indicates a paradigm that predates the rise of the fairytale and psychoanalysis. Patterns of a hypnogogic flow or destructuring and a hypnopompic flow or restructuring indicate the capacity to symbolise. Some aspects of projective identification act as a defence whereas anticipatory identification permits a prospective element. Symbol formation contains both regressive and progressive components which are essential for learning and growth.

Don't

- use jargon. Only use words that you can guarantee your reader will understand

- make bland assertions – 'extremely busy', 'well-attended', 'massive increase' – give figures
- use unsubstantiated superlatives – 'desperate need', 'absolutely unique', 'tragic waste of glorious human potential'
- assume knowledge – 'you will, I am sure, be familiar with the problems of . . .' Will they?
- patronise either the donor or the beneficiaries
- use words or concepts that will be controversial or inflammatory. Talk in a common language and build bridges from where you are to where the donor is
- use three words when one will do. Rather than saying 'From the evidence we have collected it appears that . . .' say 'Research shows that . . .'; don't say 'In the region of . . .' say 'About . . .'
- use redundant information, for example 'XXX is a registered charity and a voluntary organisation.' It will be on your letterhead
- shift fundraising responsibility – 'if you could support our appeal or know of any other company which might' – have your own clear fund-raising plan.

Sentence length

Long sentences can be a problem for readers because when the end eventually arrives, and it can be a long time in coming, they may have forgotten the beginning, especially when it contains many different ideas or many branches of a main idea, and even if they haven't forgotten they will have lost interest well before you get to the full stop. And if there's another long sentence straight after, there is a clear danger that they will give up totally because they just can't be bothered with the major mental effort you are requiring of them.

But short sentences can get on your nerves. Especially one after another. There's no variety. It's too abrupt. No flow. A real pain.

So vary the length of your sentences to achieve a balance. The average sentence length over the document should be around 15 words.

Using different media

Most funders still request applications to be sent to them, although some now accept email applications (and many accept email enquiries) or ask you to complete an online form. One or two *only* accept applications via email. However, be aware of the following.

- **Handwritten letters**: generally only use handwriting if it is for a short covering letter to someone you know. Even then, make sure it is neat and in black ink. Assume it is going to be photocopied.
- **Word processed**: you want the letter to appear personalised. This doesn't mean each letter must have different content. However, each letter should have the person's name and address typed on it and you should usually handwrite 'Dear . . .' and sign the letter yourself with your name typed underneath. (Obviously it is different if you are writing to 10,000 members.)
- **Print quality**: ensure that the letter looks well-produced.
- **Fax/email**: a few donors are happy to receive applications in one of these ways. Only use fax or email if the guide books or donors suggest them as options. When using email or filling in online applications, treat them like any other application. They will probably be printed and circulated among trustees etc.
- **CD-ROM/videos/DVDs**: these are usually best offered rather than sent. Few funders are so committed to their work that they want to listen to your appeal on the way home or watch it in the evening. If they are, they can always contact you for a copy. Also, they cannot photocopy any such media to circulate to their trustees.

  The point at which videos/DVDs come into their own is when you are making a presentation to a company for a major sponsorship or to an audience of potential donors. If you are speaking to donors, you will need back-up literature for people to take away and/or pledge forms to be signed there and then.
- **Telephone**: telephone sales techniques applied to appeals are being used more and more, especially if there is an obvious case for telephoning. This could work for alumni, membership and other constituency appeals where people expect to be asked to give, or if there is an urgent reason to give now (for example, disaster appeals).

  The telephone can also be used to follow up a written approach. A major disability charity was hosting a prestigious gala dinner at which it wished to sell tables to company executives. The organiser rang her target list of companies, explained what was going on and asked if she could fax details there and then. She rang back a short time later to see what more information the company needed, but most just agreed immediately. All the tables were booked up within two days. However, cold-calling grant-making trusts is not a good idea. They want written applications.
- **Website**: you can direct donors to your website if they need more information about your organisation and its work. But make sure that the website is well designed, with appropriate content.

7

Before you write

Once you have the ingredients of your application, a well-planned and costed project, clear outcomes and credibility facts, then you are ready to start looking for donors that want their money to achieve the same outcomes as your work. Funders estimate that between 50 and 60% of all applications they receive are immediately turned down because they do not meet clearly laid out guidelines.

Donor research

Before you write an application, you need to know to whom you are writing and what they are interested in. The perfect application to the wrong person will not get the money. An application is a communication from you (who needs the money) to the donor (who has the money). It will only be effective as a communication if it recognises the donor's particular interests and concerns.

A scatter-gun approach will produce minimal results; aim for a high success rate. The first thing to do is to find out as much as possible about the donor. Information is relatively easy to come by – from grants guides, from funders' literature (most of the larger trusts and major companies publish reports or produce information for applicants and many have a website: read the information carefully – and read between the lines), from personal contact at meetings and conferences, from gossip 'on the grapevine'. There is no excuse for sending applications to inappropriate funders. If there's a specific question you need answering, you can always telephone. So try to find out the following:

- **Who will be dealing with your application?** This is the 'correspondent', to whom you will be writing. The correspondent's job is to progress the application through the decision-making system, seeking professional or technical advice if necessary – and she or he may reject the application immediately as being of little relevance or interest. Make sure you have the correct name and job title, and that you understand the funder's interests and values. Avoid the application looking like a circular: such applications, however well designed, are almost always rejected straightaway.

- **Is there an application form?** Some funders, such as BIG and BBC Children in Need, require you to fill in an application form. The same general principles on content apply for application forms and written proposals.

- **How should the form or proposal be submitted?** While most funders still prefer you to send the hard copy of any application, refusing fax or electronic methods, others will *only* accept email applications.

- **Which budget will the money come from?** This particularly applies to companies. A donation will come from the donations budget and so you will need to write to the manager of the charitable donations. If you are proposing a formal sponsorship, this may come from the marketing budget, if which case you will be writing to the head of marketing. This can also apply to other funders. For example, some trusts fund UK-wide but have preferences for certain local areas and allocate some of their annual budget accordingly. If you operate in one of these local areas, stress the importance of your project to local people and show how it is integrated into the local community. Avoid the impression that you are a national or regional project that happens to be based in that local area.

- **What can you learn from policies, priorities and guidelines for applicants?** What is the funder interested in supporting? If you don't fit the criteria don't apply. Are there particular exclusions, types of project or expenditure that the donor will not support in any circumstances? The larger donors' websites often include up-to-date policy details as well as guidelines to applicants.

- **What grants has the funder made previously, and for what sorts of purposes?** Can you learn anything from this? For example, do they favour classical arts or community arts? Do they give a higher priority to promoting artistic excellence or involving new people in arts activities? Do they want to bring new audiences to the arts and, if so, do you need to offer full disabled access at your premises?

- **Is the funder conventional or radical in approach**? Do they appear to play safe or to take risks? Do they support campaigns? Does any of this have implications for the way in which you describe yourselves? For example, grant-making trusts are often seen as the risk-takers, the ones who will push back the boundaries of current provision by funding emerging needs and new approaches to old needs. Very few, however, report the failure of many of the projects they fund. This implies that they mainly fund projects that are more or less certain to bring in the predicted results. You need to reassure such donors that your project will bring in results, even if it is pioneering and innovative.

Fundraising is about building a partnership between two organisations that share the same objectives. The partnership operates by you doing the work and the funder giving the financial support. So you are not begging for money; you are trying to engage someone with your work.

- **What is the funder's grant range?** What is a typical grant for a project similar to your own? Are you applying for an amount the funder can realistically give? For example, a grant-making trust with an income of over £10 million does not want to give its money away in grants of £100: that would be an administrative nightmare. Its usual minimum grant will be about £500. However, for a local trust with an income of £20,000, £500 would be quite a large grant. And £500 for a small local company would be a massive grant.
- **Does the funder have advisers** who can help you informally when you are writing your application? Some funders will ask you first to submit draft proposals to an adviser who can assist with the application while remaining independent of the decision-making process.
- **Are there any connections between you and the funder?** Either a personal link or because there are particular reasons why the funder should be interested in your work. These connections may be apparent or may require some research. For example, a fundraiser for a veterinary faculty discovered that a trustee of a grant-making trust was a former graduate of the university to which she was attached. The trustee had also studied veterinary science. The trustee was promptly invited to dinner. The grant came through soon afterwards.
  Similarly, when you are writing to a company you should always make a connection between you and the company. Do you have a personal link (a member of the company's staff volunteers for your organisation, the chair of your management committee is the managing director's bridge partner), a geographical link (you and the company operate in the same area and your users are its customers) or a product link? If you can't create a link, don't bother writing to that company.

- **What is the applications procedure?** An increasing number of funders require an initial expression of interest form or, as BIG terms it, an outline proposal form, to be submitted prior to making a full application. This is to save both them and you time and effort in completing full applications where you are unlikely to receive funding. You also need to know how applications should be presented and the deadlines for receipt.

Benefits to the donor

Another aspect of donor research is establishing whether the donor might expect something in return for making the grant. In this context it is particularly important to understand the difference between sponsorship and a donation.

Sponsorship provides a direct benefit to the donor, which is the prime reason for giving support. Direct benefits include promotion and publicity, entertainment facilities and other services of commercial benefit to the sponsor.

With a donation, a donor should not normally require any significant direct benefit. Rather, donors should support the project because they believe it to be socially valuable. But it is important to be aware of some ways in which a donation can bring an indirect benefit to the donor. This can affect the way in which the proposal is presented. For example, the project might:

- provide publicity for the donation and/or identify the donor closely with the project being supported. Both provide recognition for the donor's contribution. This is especially important to companies and the National Lottery Distribution Boards (such as BIG). It is also attractive to grant-making trusts if you write up and disseminate the results of the project. The trust is then seen as funding pioneering work and promoting best practice
- deal with a problem with which the donor is also concerned. This enables the donor to achieve something without actually having to do anything (except give you the money)
- provide a better or cheaper service. The donor feels they are getting a good return on their money. On the basis that the funder has a grants budget that has to be spent, you are enabling them to spend budget money more cost-effectively.

It is important that you offer companies a benefit from their donation, whether it is better staff relations (if they support their employees' voluntary activity), an improved reputation or profile in the community (but show how are you going to achieve this), a good night out for staff, or whatever.

Irrespective of the level of benefit offered to or expected or required by the donor, there are some things you should do with all donors:

- thank them profusely and often
- report back regularly, showing them all the good things their donation has achieved
- invite them to open days and events
- introduce them to your patron, VIPs, users, etc.

These are not only good manners and an investment in a possible future grant, they also give donors a warm glow of satisfaction and a feeling of involvement.

Writing a good application

There are two golden rules when presenting your work to funders.

1 You cannot tell them everything. There isn't time and they wouldn't listen. So you have to select the points that the donor is going to be most interested in.
2 In general, don't ask funders to support your organisation. Rather, ask them to support the people you help or the work you do.

Writing the proposal is very much a matter of personal style and temperament. What works for one person will not necessarily work for another. And what works for you is what you should pay attention to. You may be able to get away with a piece of rhetoric or an impassioned plea for funds in your own handwriting or a very brief statement of your plans.

The suggestions that follow are meant as guidelines only. You can reject all of the ideas or pick up on those that seem useful to you. What is important is that you should write an application that you are happy with, that does justice to the work of your organisation and that you feel is the best way to persuade someone to support you.

The form of the application

Applications take several forms.

- **An application form supplied by the donor**. This will tell you precisely what information to supply. Use this format when required to do so. You might also wish to attach a covering letter or supporting information, although your case is likely to be judged on what you have put on the form.

Some application forms are extremely detailed. Some lottery boards, for example, have forms over 20 pages. Just because you are filling out a form doesn't mean that you switch off your fundraising brain. Try to communicate the important needs you are meeting, your effectiveness in meeting them and the cost-effectiveness of your approach.

This applies equally to online applications, which usually also involve completing a form. Avoid the temptation to abbreviate and write in a different style simply because it is an online application. It will almost certainly be printed off to be assessed at some stage. Formatting diffi-culties and compatibility can also create problems, which you have to work through.

- **An application letter** in which you set out your case and attach sup-porting information as required. This format will be appropriate in most circumstances and is covered in detail in this chapter.

- **A project proposal and a covering letter**, together with supporting information. This follows on from the above. Dividing the application into two parts, a project proposal and a letter, has certain advantages. The letter can contain personal information – previous contact with the donor, particular reasons why the donor might be interested and a project summary. The project proposal will be more formal and factual; the letter more upbeat, selling the idea of support. This format is especially useful for longer applications or where you are sending a standard proposal to a large number of donors. However, there is the danger that you can use it as an excuse to provide too much information and that not everyone will read enough of the proposal to get a proper picture.

- **An initial expression of interest** followed by a more detailed formal proposal (if requested). This seems to be an increasingly popular method with funders, and is used by some lottery boards as well as some large trusts such as Tudor. Once you have submitted the initial expression of interest (a letter or a standard form), the funder will let you know whether to submit a full application.

The information you supply will be assessed by the grants secretary, trust director, corporate affairs manager (or whoever) and put forward as a summary and recommendation to the grants committee or trustees, who will then make the decision. This is the most usual procedure for all but the smallest grant sources. So, it is possible that the people making the final decisions will not read your letter and other beautifully constructed prose.

All they may see is a summary of your proposal. Therefore you must make a good, clear case which can be easily understood and summarised.

Suggested structure for an application letter

- Project title
- Proposal summary
- Introduction: who you are
- The problem or need
- What you will do
- How you will do it
- How you will know if you've been successful
- How much you need to do it
- How you will get the money
- The request
- Why the donor might be interested
- Where the money will come from in the future
- Signing off

The structure of the application

Whatever form of proposal you produce, it has to fulfil certain functions. It must inform the reader of who you are, what you intend to do and why; it also has to say how much money you need and what you intend to spend it on. It should do this in a clear and logical way. Some of the elements you might use in constructing your proposal are detailed below.

1 The title

It is often a good idea to give your proposal a title, particularly if you can do this in a catchy phrase that captures the essence of what you want to do.

2 A summary

For a longer proposal, a summary can be very important. It presents the essence of what the proposal is about, and allows the reader to determine whether it is likely to be of interest. The summary may be presented in a covering letter or the first paragraph of the application letter. It should be clear, concise and specific. It should describe who you are, the scope of your project and the projected cost. The summary is the first part of your proposal that will be read – and it may be the last. Make sure that you follow the normal fundraising rules, even in the summary paragraph. Be positive and upbeat and state that something really good will happen as a result of this project.

Key question

Who are this lot – and can I trust them?

3 The introduction: who you are

Many proposals tell little or nothing about the applicant organisation and speak only about the project or programme to be conducted. If you are a nationally known organisation, you can state who you are in a line or a sentence. Usually you need to provide more information. Proposals are often funded on the basis of the reputation of the applicant organisation and its key people, as well as on the basis of the proposed project. Use this section to build your credibility as an organisation that deserves to be supported.

Here are some of the things you can say about your organisation in your introduction.

- Any previous connection with the funding source. Whether you have had a grant before or have applied and been turned down.
- Your organisation's goals or objectives and the basic thrust of your work.
- How you got started.
- How long you have been around.
- Anything unique about the way you got started, or the fact that you pioneered a new type of activity.
- Some of your most significant accomplishments as an organisation or, if you are a new organisation, some of the significant accomplishments of your staff in their previous roles.
- What support you have received from other organisations and prominent individuals (accompanied perhaps by letters of endorsement, which can be put in an appendix).

You are not putting down history for the sake of history, rather you are doing this to build your credibility. You are trying to show that you are a safe pair of hands, that you are (hopefully) an imaginative and exciting organisation to be associated with, and that you will continue to deliver a high quality of service.

Key question

Who are their users – and what is their (the users') problem?

---

4 The problem statement or assessment of need: why something needs to be done

In the introduction you have said who you are. Now you will home in on the specific problem(s) that you want to solve through the proposed project. There are several common errors that applicants make at this point:

- Painting too broad a picture of all the ills plaguing people, the local community or the wider world. For example, 'X is a rural area that has been classified as disadvantaged due to high unemployment, low stock of local authority accommodation and little to no leisure facilities'. They do not narrow down to specific, solvable problems. They give the impression that it will take a hundred times the requested budget even to begin to deal with the identified problems. This is overkill. You may need to confine your definition of the problem so as to allow you to propose a solution. For example '80% of children who attend the group come from low income families and so have no opportunity to access recreational facilities'. You are then showing how you will make a positive impact within a reasonable time and with reasonable resources.
- Going on about the organisation and its needs. 'The community centre roof is falling in so please help us put a new one on.' 'All our play equipment is broken and our subs don't cover the replacement cost.' 'Our staff are overworked.' Although these may be the immediate reasons for your fundraising, always present your proposals on the basis of your users, their needs, their hopes and aspirations. Fixing the centre roof is not done just so you have a nice waterproof centre, but to enable the activities to take place inside.
- Concentrating on the service the applicant wants to provide rather than why they want to provide it. The letter launches in with something like:

'We want to provide a desperately needed new information line for at risk women' and then explains in great detail how the service will be provided, managed and financed, but at no point does it say why there is a need for the service in the first place and the really important changes the service will help make in the lives of those using it.

You need to document the problem. How do you know that a problem exists? As one major trust puts it: 'What is the need for the work and how have you identified it? Who have you consulted about the project and what did this tell you?'

Furthermore, don't assume that everybody knows this is a problem. Use your own or other people's information to strengthen your case. For example, which of the following do you think is more convincing:

- 'It stands to reason that children whose parents cannot read or write will do badly at school'
- 'A recent Joseph Rowntree Foundation report on growing up with parents who have learning difficulties showed conclusively that "children's destinies are not fixed by having a mother or father with learning difficulties". The report went on to argue that . . .'

Assume that the funder is intensely sceptical about the need for your project. What can you do to prove them wrong? Most funders will want hard evidence of the need for your project – bland assertions and generalised statements will not get past them.

Notwithstanding the above, don't go overboard and fill your proposal with tables, charts and graphs. These will interfere with the flow of the argument. Figures are only helpful if they support an argument. If you must use extensive statistics, put them in an appendix, but put the key figures into your statement of the problem.

When explaining why something needs to be done now, you need to do the following:

- Make a logical connection between your organisation's background and the problems and needs with which you propose to work.
- Define clearly the problems with which you intend to work.
- Support the existence of the problem by evidence. Statistics are one type of evidence. You may also get advice from groups in your community

concerned about the problem, from prospective clients, from other organisations working in your community and from professionals in the field.

- Make sure that what you want to do is workable and directly addresses the defined problem. That it can be done within a reasonable time, by you, and with a reasonable amount of money.
- Show how something must be done *now*. If you can't give the application a sense of urgency, the funder will turn to one of the many that can.

Key question

How will they make life better for their users?

5 Your objectives and outcomes: what you intend to do about the problem and what the work will achieve

Clearly, if you have defined a problem then your proposals should offer a way of helping to relieve it. Show that you have a clear plan to address the problems and issues you have highlighted. Specify the outcomes of the work, the difference your project will make. Give numbers of beneficiaries and who they are. Set yourself targets for what you propose to do so that you can give the funder a clear idea of what will happen and when. To quote from BBC Children in Need guidelines:

> . . .we look for information which is clear, realistic and focused on changes for the better in people's lives. Try to avoid vague or unrealistic statements and be as specific as you can, e.g. instead of telling us the children will be 'happier'; outline the ways in which you will see their lives improve – such as increased sociability, language skills and positive relationships.

For example, if the problem you identify is a high incidence of vandalism by young people in your community (substantiated, of course), then an objective of your programme should be a reduction of the incidence of such vandalism. Outcomes may then be changes in young people's attitude and behaviour, improved relationships between the young people and the rest of the community. If the problem is long-term unemployment, then an objective is getting long-term unemployed people into jobs. Outcomes may include increasing beneficiaries' work skills, increased motivation and aspirations and better qualifications.

Distinguish between objectives (what you aim to achieve) and methods (how you will do it – see the next point). If you are having difficulty in defining your objectives and outcomes, try projecting your organisation a year or two into the future. What differences would you hope to see between then and now? What changes will have occurred? These changed dimensions may be the objectives and outcomes of your programme.

Also, and crucially, try to show that your users – or the intended bene-ficiaries – have had a major input into developing the ideas and plans for the project. Have they been involved from the outset, or has there just been a token consultation towards the end?

It is worth examining your objectives in a little more detail. Some pro-grammes may create very short-term jobs for people and attract those who are best able to find work by themselves. Even if they reduce the unemployment problem in the short term, after a year or two the problem will be back, as bad or worse than ever. You should be concerned about the quality of your work as well as the quantity (the number of people you are helping).

Just as when describing the problem or need, you need to be as precise as you can in describing the extent of the service being provided, and the impact on those you are helping. For example, in considering a project targeting families who are locked into a cycle of debt and dependence on benefits:

> Our pilot project showed how we could help people break out of this cycle. As a result of the XXX Initiative, P% of those attending were still in training or education after six months and Q% had already found full or part-time work. As a result, their household income has risen by R%. More importantly, they now feel they have control over their own lives and futures.

You can take it further to demonstrate the cost-effectiveness and value for money your project represents. Many grantmakers are now judging appli-cations on the impact or outcome of the work and the value for the money they are putting up.

Set specific targets for the project. On the above example you could say something like:

> By the end of the three-year project, we expect a further W people to have gone through our X programme. Of these, Y will then go onto formal job training or into further education and Z will be in full or part-time work.

This will give you a clear basis by which to measure the success of your work and reassure the funder that the project is well planned and thought through.

Key question

How do I know that it will work?

---

6 The methods: how you will attempt to do it

You have already stated who you are, the problem you want to work with, your objectives and outcomes (which promise a solution to, or reduction of, the problem). Now you are going to explain how you intend to bring about these results.

You will need to describe the methods you will use and the activities you will conduct. You will also need to persuade the funder that they will work. You can do this by demonstrating that:

- this project is based on a successful model developed elsewhere
- the outputs are clearly defined and realistic
- it is a natural extension of work you have already undertaken, so it is not some great leap in the dark
- it fits well with your organisation's other activities
- you have successfully managed similar projects in the past
- you have experienced and well-qualified people to run the project
- you have the users' support and commitment and they have been involved in the project's planning
- it has the backing of key people and agencies, which can act as an independent verification of the project plan

- it is well thought through, with clear targets and regular review processes
- your past work gives confidence that this new project is well within your capabilities.

The informed donor may want to know why you have selected these methods, particularly for an innovative project. This requires you to know a good deal about other similar projects. Who else is working on the problem and where? Are there similar projects providing similar services in your area? If so, how do you fit in with their work? What information helped you decide this was the best way to address the identified problem? Did you consider any other ways of making the difference? In other words, can you justify and substantiate your approach?

Key question

How will they know whether they are being successful?

---

7 Monitoring and evaluation: how you will measure performance

A key element of modern voluntary sector management – as well as one of the most important concerns for funders – is that of monitoring and evaluation. Put simply, being busy is not enough; funders want to know that you are being effective. You need to be able to provide evidence to a funder that you are making a difference. The outcomes you have already stated should be measurable in some way. You have to state how you will assess the progress of the work against these outcomes. This is done using outcome indicators, which can be quantitative (where you count the number of things that happen, such as the number of people who found jobs following some specific training) or qualitative (where you assess people's views and experiences, such as how safe older people feel going out at night).

Increasingly funders are asking for targets (or milestones) to be identified during the application process. These enable you not only to ensure that you are carrying out the activities planned but that these activities are achieving the expected results.

Basically, monitoring is about getting information; evaluation is making decisions in the light of this information. Monitoring can take many forms, including interviews, questionnaires, surveys and consultation meetings. Evaluation generally requires a manager or, more usually, a group of people to look at the feedback you get from your monitoring, assessing the points and issues it raises and deciding whether you need to do anything differently.

From a funder's viewpoint, there are three key issues in the monitoring and evaluation process:

- You are taking user comment and feedback very seriously. Just as you have involved users in defining the need and drawing up the project proposal, you also need to show that you will be involving them in the ongoing management and development of the project. It is not enough to assume that because you haven't had many complaints things are going OK, or that because you are getting enough people along then you must be providing a good service. Funders want to see that you will be actively seeking out verification of all of this.
- You don't just carry on regardless. Despite your best endeavours, things don't always turn out as you planned. You need to show that you will be able to stay on top of people and events, and respond to situations as they develop rather than trying to make everything fit a pre-determined model. Monitoring and evaluation processes give you this reality check.
- The knowledge and information gathered as you run the project will be fed into the development of the project and, indeed, the wider organisation. You will be learning a lot of really valuable information, both about the way in which you work and your users' ongoing needs; you want to show how all of this will feed into your project and organisational planning.

Monitoring and evaluation isn't about tying you down to the last penny or ensuring that you deal with exactly the same number of people in exactly the same way as you said you were going to in your funding proposal (although there is an important element of accountability in all this). Funders would much prefer that you were clear in what you are trying to achieve but also honest in your assessment of performance. If it becomes clear that you should be doing things in a slightly different way from that originally envisaged, then tell the funders how you have learned these lessons and why a modified approach would deliver better results for you and your users. They are usually happy to agree to their money being used in a slightly different way if it means the end results are more likely to be achieved.

You need to tell the funders how you intend to gather information during the course of the project and how you will evaluate it. For larger funding applications, it can often be worth setting up a small project steering committee, drawing in the organisation, some partner agencies and some users. Basically, you need to show that:

- you will be obtaining useful and reliable information
- this information will inform the development of the project
- any problems will be identified early and will be acted upon
- user comment and criticism will be sought out and used as a key management and development tool.

Key question

How much is it going to cost?

---

8 The budget: how much you will need to do this work

Fundraising is really about selling an idea rather than asking for money. It is primarily about showing how you can change things for the better. However, once you have sold the idea to someone with the means and inclination to support you, you then need to get down to the business of asking for money.

The budget is simply a statement of what you intend to spend on the project. It will include the direct project expenditure and an allocation of overhead costs. In the application you may want to give a total budget figure, or you might break it down into smaller items according to what you think the particular donor is interested in (for example, a particular project, idea or piece of equipment). Either way, the budget should show how the whole thing fits together. See chapter 5 for more information.

Be confident about money. If you have shown that you are a good organisation, that you are responding to an important need in a sensible and appropriate way, that the funder can take further confidence from your excellent track record and experience of this kind of work and that you can point to a well-costed budget – then if that is what the project costs, that is what it costs. Don't be apologetic for asking for the money you need to do a good job. Tell it how it is. When looking at a budget, funders will consider issues such as whether:

- the budget has been calculated in a clear and logical way that has taken all relevant costs into account
- it has been put together by someone who understands the problem
- it is based on experience of budgeting for other projects
- the costs are reasonable for this type of work and will allow you to provide an appropriate level of service
- you have not budgeted in a way that will compromise quality.

If you are applying for a grant over several years, inflation can pose a problem. There are two ways of tackling this. Firstly, you can allow for inflation at a guessed rate; secondly you can compute your own budget at present costs and ask for an inflation allowance to be added each year according to the prevailing level. If you are in doubt, consult the funder, who may have specific ways of dealing with this.

Key question

Where are they getting the money from?

---

9 Funding plan

If you are only applying to a donor for part of the money you need, explain where you intend to obtain the balance. The funder will be asking two key questions:

- **What is the organisation's track record in fundraising?** What does this tell me about its ability to get money for this project? For example, if you have raised around £50,000 a year from grant-making trusts for the last six years and you are currently seeking support for a £30,000 project, the donor you are writing to will be pretty confident in your ability to raise the full amount and will contribute accordingly. If you have never raised a penny and now expect to get £100,000 over the next year, this looks like wishful thinking unless you can make a convincing case otherwise.
- **Who else has put money in?** The more money you have raised or been promised from elsewhere, the more confidence this funder will have in your ability to get the project fully funded.

If you are applying for a piece of equipment or a capital project, it's not just a matter of showing how you can raise the money to buy the equipment. You must also demonstrate that you have the resources to use it. Donors don't like paying for a building or an expensive piece of equipment only to find it lying idle as you can't afford to use it. You need to demonstrate how you intend to meet these running costs.

Key question

How much do they want from us?

---

10 The request: how much to ask for

At this stage, many applications tail off into a murmur that any contribution would be gratefully received. This is partly due to an embarrassment about asking for money. It also stems from a lack of confidence about exactly how much to ask for.

Going back to first principles, fundraising is about making a good case, selling a cause. Once the case is made and the donor accepts the importance of the project, making a grant is something that is done willingly because the donor wants to help.

The only question is how much to give. Donors vary; some prefer you to ask for a specific amount (some even specify how much) while, at the other extreme, there are funders that ask you to leave the figure entirely to them. Most funders are somewhere in the middle, so it is usually helpful if you make a specific request rather than ask the donor to decide what is appropriate. Of course, before you do this you need to know how much the donor is able to give – the total amount available and a typical size of grant made in the past to similar organisations for similar purposes. You can then assess the likely grant range from this donor and ask for a specific amount. You can make this suggestion in a number of ways:

- **Ask directly for a specific sum** ('I would like to ask you for a one-off grant of £5,000', or 'Could you support us with £2,500 for three years', or whatever).
- **Show how much other trusts have given or has been committed** ('The Garfield Weston Foundation has already given us £10,000'). This will

indicate that you expect a similar amount from the trust to which you are currently writing.

- **Say how many trusts you are writing to and for how much** ('I am writing to you and nine other trusts asking for a total of £42,000'). This again gives the donor an idea of how much you are expecting it to give (£5,000–£10,000 in this example), but also allows for flexibility. You can even append a list of the donors you are approaching. They may know one another and discuss your application and the contribution each might make if they are particularly impressed with it.
- **Provide a shopping list** (£12,000 for the project itself, £3,000 for the research, £3,000 for the publication, £2,000 for the evaluation, etc.). The donor can then choose what to support, based on its preferences and budget.

You also need to show how the funder's grant fits into the overall picture. So you should say how much you need in total, where it is coming from and what you expect that donor to give. For example: 'We need to raise £210,000. Our members have already committed £60,000 and the health authority has agreed to match this amount. We expect to raise a further £40,000 from fundraising events, £20,000 from local and national companies and £30,000 from grant-making trusts. I am therefore writing to ask you for . . .'. This will give the funder more confidence that you know what you are doing and that you can raise the necessary money.

Key question

So why does it interest us?

---

11 The rationale: why the donor might be interested

There are many reasons why the donor might be interested in your proposal, such as:

- you are running a good project which falls within the donor's stated policies and priorities
- you have already received a grant from the donor, and a further grant is an investment in your success
- the donor had a known interest in, or a connection with, the problem or cause

- there is a personal connection, which it will pay to highlight
- there is a payback for the donor in the form of good publicity.

Whatever the reason, you may want to mention it in the application (or the covering letter or a conversation with the donor). This is particularly important when you are approaching a company, which will want to know what PR or other commercial benefit it will get from its support.

Key question

If the project is there for the long term, how is the organisation going to continue to pay for it?

---

12 Where will the money come from in future?

Another important consideration is what you intend to do when the grant you are seeking runs out. Is your project time-limited, say three years or less? If so, you don't have to worry about getting funding beyond then. However, often you are trying to get a new project going on the basis that if it works you will want it to continue for as long as necessary (and certainly beyond three years). Given that most funders will not give grants for more than three years, what happens when their funding runs out?

You need to think about this at the outset, as no funding source wants to be locked into supporting a project forever. One way used to be to get a commitment from a statutory authority to take over the project once it had proved itself; but with cutbacks in public spending, this has become increasingly difficult, if not impossible. So what are the options?

- If the statutory authority will not definitely commit itself to funding the whole project, then it may at least indicate a willingness to consider a funding application if the project proves successful.
- You may be able to show that the project fits in with a statutory service's priorities and that you expect to be able to run it on a contract basis.
- The project may generate an income of its own (for example you can build in a charging structure to users or another body, which will grow to cover the project's costs within the lifespan of the grant).

- You are developing your general fundraising or income-generating activities and expect to be able to pay for the project – or at least a substantial proportion of the costs – from within your own resources.
- Over the lifetime of the grant you will be aiming to double your membership to bring an additional £X a year into your organisation. Some of this can be transferred to paying for the project from year four onwards.

It may be that you use a combination of the above or have some other scheme of your own. The key thing to do is to think about it now and show the funder that you are planning ahead. You may not be certain that you will be able to obtain funding in the way you suggest, but at least you will have thought about the problem at an early stage and provided some reassurance to those who would like to fund you.

Also, it gives you a fundraising plan to be getting on with.

In fact, many funders like the idea of giving grants on a tapering basis – for example £15,000 in year 1, £12,000 in year 2 and £8,000 in year 3. As their grant reduces, other money comes into the project. Asking for money on this basis can help show that you are confident of bringing in this additional money, and that in turn gives the funder confidence in the long-term viability of your work.

13 The signatory

Who signs the application can be important. If the donor recognises or knows the applicant, this can be helpful. The following are possible signatories:

- the project leader
- the fundraiser or development officer
- the organisation's director
- the chair of the trustees or management committee
- an appeals patron
- an expert or prominent personality with some connection with the cause.

Who is the best person for the job depends very much on the nature of the body you are approaching. It is up to you to decide who will be the best signatory to the application. But beware of the following:

- You write saying that you are doing so at the suggestion of a prominent person (connected with you and known to the funder). This can imply that that person is too busy to be able or want to make the application in person.
- Follow-up information and contact will be with another person. This again implies that the person signing the letter is too important or too busy to be concerned with following it up. As a general principle any signatory should be prepared, at least, to attend a follow-up meeting with the donor (diary permitting) to discuss the grant.
- The signatory has a job title which appears too junior – fundraising assistant or assistant to the director, for example. Again, this implies that you are not treating the application seriously. If you are given the responsibility for signing the letter and your job title is inadequate, then get promoted – or at least get it agreed that you can use a more appropriate job title when signing fundraising letters.
- The signatory is a fundraising consultant acting on your behalf. There are two problems here:
  (i) The consultant will almost certainly become a professional fund-raiser under the terms of the Charities Act and will have to make some rather clumsy-looking declarations about how he or she is being paid for the work.
  (ii) Many funders refuse to consider appeals from a third party on behalf of a charity. Even if they don't rule you out on these grounds, donors respond best to direct requests, even though the approach may have been put together with professional advice.

The length of the application

You cannot tell donors everything. You don't have the time and they won't read it. You just need to tell them enough. Most donors do not say: 'We generally expect an application for under £20,000 to be up to six sides of A4 and applications for over £30,000 to be up to and occasionally more than 10 sides of A4' (although this statement was taken from a trust's guidelines).

It is difficult enough reading 30 applications each day, every day – which is what many donors have to do. Put yourself in their position. You would pick up an application, look at who it was from, read the first paragraph and then possibly decide that the application was not really worth bothering with. If you did read all of it, you might skip through much of the text simply because there was so much to read.

On the other hand, if the application was clear, to the point and brief it would be so much easier to absorb the information. Donors are not paying you for the words you write. So you don't have to provide a lot of words to get a lot of money. They can always ask you for further information if they think it necessary.

Nor is it a case of 'never mind the quality, feel the width'. You have to show what you are doing, give evidence that it is an exciting project that meets a real and important need and that you can make an impact.

- Try to keep the application to two pages for a grant-making trust and one page for a company. This means that it can be easily photocopied and stands less chance of being summarised and possibly misrepresented by someone else. Obviously, for a very major project you might want to go into more detail, but in such cases you can write a much shorter summary proposal.
- If in doubt, leave it out. Each point must add something to your case. If it doesn't, it is making a negative impact by obscuring those parts of the application that do.
- You can always supply more detail in an attachment, although this may not be read. Or you can indicate that further information is available on request, which funders will seldom ask for. Or the funder will ask to meet you; any discussion will generate far more useful and revealing information about the proposal and your competence than anything you put in writing.

Don't rely on the attachments. Assume the only things funders read are the letter and budget. They should have a full understanding of who you are, what you want to do, why it's important and what it will cost. If you keep writing in the letter 'For further information see attached', they probably won't.

Always attach a budget for the project, an annual report and a set of accounts. Over and above that, think what the donors will want to know and what they will need to know before they give their support. Don't overload the system by sending everything. This is a waste of money and paper and will cost more to post. And not all the extra material will be photocopied for the trustees or grants committee members.

All attachments are fundraising documents. The same rules that apply to writing your fundraising letter apply to the attachments (short sentences, easy to read, lots of sub-headings, etc.). If they are not easy to read or are packed with jargon, either rewrite them or leave them out.

Back-up information

You might want to include, or a funder may request, any or all of these:

- Your organisation's annual report and accounts, or a leaflet containing the information in an abridged form (this would include photographs of your work wherever possible).
- A detailed budget for the project.
- A detailed plan for the project.
- Visual material, such as photographs of the project in action or architectural drawings for a building project.
- A background briefing on the need for the project (to include key statistics which bolster your case).
- A case study or several examples of the problem or what you can achieve.
- A list of donors and contributors.
- A fundraising plan (where and from whom you intend to get the money).
- Curricula vitae of the key personnel involved in the project.
- Job descriptions of new posts being created
- A list of trustees, patrons, vice-presidents or other key supporters.
- Letters of endorsement from prominent people/other funders/users/ beneficiaries.
- A quotes sheet where users, community leaders and other notables say really positive things about you.
- Photocopies of press cuttings.

Sending your application

What to do with your application

Once you've written your application, you need to think about and plan how, when and to whom to send it. You may have targeted a number of potentially interested sources and need several grants to make up the total cost of the project. Who should you approach first? And for how much? How can you maximise the chances of meeting your fundraising target? And how can you make sure that you raise the money you need within, often tight, deadlines?

There are no specific answers to these questions. It is as much a matter of your judgement and style as anything else. But the following points may help.

1 Apply immediately

Applications for small sums to the smaller trusts can usually be sent whenever you like. Many of these trusts meet infrequently (often only once or twice a year) and it may be some time before you hear the result of your appeal. The sooner you get these applications out the better.

However, small local grants can be useful in levering out large national ones. The fact of the endorsement is probably more useful to you than the amount they give, as it gives confidence to larger, national funders that those on the ground know, like and trust you. But remember that national trusts will only know you have got local money if you tell them.

2 The blanket approach

Suppose you have identified 30 sources as being potentially interested in your work; you might then send out all 30 applications at once. The advantage of this is that you will have asked 30 people to support you, and they can then decide whether to do so. The disadvantage is that your appeal may not be as strong as if you had adopted the step-by-step approach (see below).

You might state that you are approaching a number of sources and even name some. You might indicate in some way how much you would like each to give (for example 'We are writing to you and eight other major trusts asking for a total of £30,000.').

Some donors will not reply. Some will acknowledge receipt of your application and that will be the last you hear. Some will want further information. A few might request a meeting. Some will simply send you a cheque if your application is successful.

You can use their responses to improve your chances. If one of your top prospects says 'no', it may be worth politely finding out why, possibly asking for a meeting or a visit so that you can explain the importance of your work in greater depth. You may be able to turn a 'no' into a 'yes' in this way. In any case you will accumulate information about that funder's approach to grantmaking, which will improve your chances of success next time around.

If you have been successful with one trust you can send a follow-up letter to some of the other trusts that have not yet reached a decision, outlining the progress of the appeal. This reminds them of your appeal as well as providing information that might enhance your chances.

If you fall just short of your target, don't keep trying to find yet another untapped source of money. Go back to a few of your key supporters, say how successful you have been and see if there is the possibility of topping up their support with a further small grant.

3 The step-by-step approach

Here you identify from your list of potential sources a few which you believe are more likely to be interested in you and which have the resources to make a substantial grant. If you are applying for a larger grant from a statutory source, it is always important to do this first, and to get some commitment before approaching others for support. Most non-statutory funders would want to know you had got the maximum from any statutory source before approaching them.

How you approach your major donors will depend on their application procedures, how well you are known to them and whether they have supported you previously. You may be able to arrange a meeting to discuss your proposal; you may want to find out first about the grant cycle, when applications are due in and when they will be considered.

Most of the major grant-making trusts are based in London and the south east of England. That's fine if you are also based there, but most of us aren't. So before writing to such a trust check to see if there are any local trusts that you can approach first. They may be big; they may be small. However, the point is not necessarily to get huge sums from them; rather, you are in effect trying to say to the London-based trust: 'You may not have heard of us because we are not based in your area. However, the XXX Trust, which is based in our area and is in a position to know, thinks we are marvellous and has just given us £1,000. Therefore you can take confidence from this support.' Obviously you don't actually write this! The grant from a local trust is acting like a letter of reference.

A similar result may be achieved when approaching larger, well-known trusts that have a regional structure. For example, Lloyds TSB, Esmée Fairbairn Charitable Trust and BBC Children in Need have regional offices and assessors. It can be worth contacting such trusts early in the process to see if they will commit to giving you a grant. A commitment from one of these trusts can be very helpful in persuading national foundations to support you, as they will know that, for example, Lloyds TSB will have assessed your application using its regional administrators.

Many funders are operating what is, in effect, a pledge system. They commit to giving you a certain sum on the understanding that the total amount is raised by a certain date. It is fairly straightforward for you to operate a similar system. You can write along the lines of: 'We are aiming to raise a total of £75,000 by September 2010. Will you commit to giving £10,000 on the basis that the total sum is raised by then?'

They don't actually send you the £10,000 until you can confirm that you have raised the other £65,000. However, you can use their commitment to obtain similar pledges from other funders: 'We are aiming to raise a total of £75,000 by September 2010. We have already firm commitments of support totalling £40,000. We therefore only need a further £35,000. Will you commit to giving £10,000 on the basis that the total sum is raised by then?'

Do all you can to get your large grants committed. Once you have your first grant, everything becomes much easier. Your target is reduced; you have an endorsement for what you are doing; and your confidence grows. This makes it more likely that others will agree to support you.

Whatever you do, make sure that for each approach you mention an aspect of your fundraising strategy. Ask for support at a specific level and put this into the context of your overall fundraising plans for the project. Always quote the highest figure you need, showing how much has been raised and how much you still need.

4 The delayed approach

In most applications you will ask for money. But there are other possibilities. You can send an outline of your proposals and ask for a meeting to discuss your ideas. This is usually only worthwhile where you are already known to the donor, where it has regional offices or specialist advisers. Otherwise, funders normally prefer a full written proposal in the first instance –although, as mentioned earlier (see page 5), several larger funders now require a preliminary expression of interest or outline proposal form prior to submitting a full application.

You can try to get potential funders to visit you. Open days, launches and other, particularly prestigious, events can be suitable opportunities. Some projects, such as city farms, have a product which is inherently attractive to donors, and experience shows that most of the people who visit eventually decide to give financial support. In such circumstances, the challenge is to find ways of getting them to accept an invitation to visit you.

You can try to get yourself known in the grant-making world before you actually apply. This means:

- meeting grants administrators and advisers at events and conferences and making sure you introduce yourself
- sending out your annual report (for information purposes only) to potential supporters

- seeking and getting publicity in the media
- building your trustee, patron and supporter base so that you create wider contacts for your organisation.

It is hard to obtain substantial support for a project when you have never received support before. This may mean presenting more modest needs now and building on this over time. It also means being clear about which funders you are targeting over the next five years or so and making sure you think strategically about how you will do this.

What to do after submitting the application

Mostly you will do nothing, except wait for a response. You can chase up your letter with a phone call to find out if it has arrived, when it will be considered and whether the funder requires any further information. This, at least, has the advantage of putting a human voice to a written application. But you need to do this carefully. There is a danger of appearing to hassle, which funders will resent.

When you receive a positive reply, say 'thank you' immediately. Put the donor on a mailing list to receive information on your work (such as annual reports and copies of your publications). Note any conditions of the grant (for example, terms for spending the money, reporting and audit requirements).

Keep good records of your contacts. Add information from your refusals as well as your successes. They may give you reasons for turning you down. These may help you next time, although what they say may be out of politeness rather than the bare truth. When you do re-apply, remind the funder that you have applied before. Remember that the bodies that have supported you this time are quite likely to want to support you again (unless they have a specific policy of not doing so).

You should consider when and how next to approach them. As most grantmakers work on annual cycles, you may decide to go back for more support next year. As a rule, never apply to the same funder more than once in their financial year.

Anybody who has turned you down should be seen as a possibility for future funding (unless there are clear reasons why they will never support you). You have decided they are likely to be interested. The only problem is that they have not yet come to the same conclusion. Your challenge is to present a better case next time or even the time after. Persistence can pay.

A first application should be seen as the beginning, not the end, of the process. Success in raising money depends as much on building relationships, and not giving up, as on writing a good application for a good project.

Timing and timescale

One reason many applications fail is that they are made too late. The time to think about applying is well before you need the money. This means that planning ahead is vital. Raising money to extricate your organisation from a financial crisis is by far the most difficult form of fundraising.

There are various stages in the application process, each with a timescale attached:

- Getting known and getting to know potential supporters.
- Building credibility with a donor, so that the donor will be happy to give you a grant rather than a token donation.
- Developing your fundraising ideas and completing a written application. This might include a period of discussion with potential donors.
- Submitting a formal application.
- Assessing the application and making a recommendation to the trustees or grants committee.
- The timescale for the funder's decision at a trustee or grants committee meeting.
- Communication of the decision to the applicant, which may require an acceptance by the applicant of the terms and conditions of the grant before the money can be paid over.

The first two stages can take years, but time spent on building credibility is never wasted. The subsequent phases also take time. The trustees or grants committee may only meet quarterly and may require applications to be submitted at least one month in advance. The grants budget at the next trustee meeting may already be fully allocated and the applicant might only stand any real chance if the application is deferred until a subsequent meeting.

Organisations in receipt of local authority funding must apply in the late summer for grants for the year beginning the following May. And they may be wise to start preliminary discussions for the next year's grant at about the time that the current year's grant is confirmed.

Of course, there will always be emergencies or projects where the need was unforeseen, which require funding immediately. The point is that if you have already developed good relationships with potential funders, securing emergency funding is that much easier. Conversely, if you haven't done the preparatory work it is difficult, and often impossible, to get funded at short notice, however desperate the need.

10

Worked examples

This chapter analyses some genuine applications which have been sent to real funders. We aim to be constructively critical and suggest ways in which they could be improved. Each application letter is reproduced, although some have been slightly modified to disguise the true identity of the organisation. We also provide a commentary to highlight some key points.

There are a number of lessons to be gained from reading through these annotated examples:

- Once an application is written, it is often easy to improve on it. Read your first draft, get others to read it, and produce a much better second (and final) draft.
- Many applications that are sent are not particularly good. They are impersonal circulars, impassioned pleas without sufficient evidence to make a good case, a hotchpotch of half-thought-through ideas; or they are sent to someone who is unlikely to be interested (the applications here are generally much better than most). Writing a good application gets you off to a good start.
- Read through a range of applications. That puts you in a similar position to a donor – you will have a lot to read about projects you know little about. Which would you fund if you had a limited grants budget at your disposal? Understanding the process from the donor's point of view can only be helpful.
- Finding the correct people to write to is as important as getting the message right.

All the examples shown here are good attempts by people working for successful projects that they believe in. We hope they take our comments in the positive context we intended!

Example 1 – Jargon will get you nowhere

This application comes from a very committed and low-cost project. It is also nice and short. However, sadly, it doesn't really tell you anything, or at least nothing that is substantiated. It is simply a series of assertions – generally in some kind of management speak – that leave the reader none the wiser.

25th January

Dear Secretary

We are writing to ask for a few minutes of your time to read of our work and of our aims and objectives for the challenging year ahead.

Our small charitable Foundation is trying to raise funds to enable us to both continue and enlarge projects already established around the World, also to break into new horizons where we feel we can make a difference to the lives of those who face poverty, disadvantage, and physical or mental distress and be an enabler in them achieving real improvement in the quality of their lives.

In short our Hopes and Dreams Projects aim to provide Skills Transfer and encourage Social Development. We have maintained a high degree of Local Empowerment, Ownership and Involvement and our innovative projects have realised significant benefits relative to outlay; on hand-over, each project has the initial grounding to become self-sustaining. Our Foundation has been on time with all targets set to date, and will endeavour to continue this example. Evaluation methods continue to be in place both before and after hand-over.

We have the necessary Management Structure and have an Equal Opportunities Statement and a Mission Statement in place. Computers have made it possible for mass production of letters such as this, but we do assure you our greatest wish is to be as personal as possible in every project we undertake giving each recipient of our services the respect and love they so richly deserve.

If you would like to see photographs of our 'special' people, both young and elderly, please do consider telephoning to speak to me, I would like the opportunity of speaking to you.

Finally, we do not employ computer wizards, and our office work is carried out voluntarily. Much time is spent on sorting letters, but human errors do occur, I do hope very much that you do not receive more than one letter, please forgive us if you do. Postage money has been donated. We really would appreciate any financial help that you may be able to give, no matter how small.

Yours very truly

Helen Bateman

For example, what does it mean 'to provide Skills Transfer and encourage Social Development'? Even if you get past the jargon of 'realised significant benefits relative to outlay', where is any evidence or illustration of any of the points made in paragraph three? Why should the funder trust you simply because you know your way around some voluntary sector catch phrases? Significantly, where is there any evidence of meaningful local partnership, the absolute essential of any non-UK work?

This letter will make complete sense to the person who wrote it, but to few others. It's always a good idea to give your application to someone outside your organisation to read before you send it off. It is not very easy when you are committed to and know a lot about a subject to see it from the non-expert's perspective. Jargon can be the death of an application; it certainly is in this case.

Also, this letter is clearly a circular. The original has a photocopied signature – which is a bit of a giveaway – but the whole tone is impersonal. There is no mention of the funder, nor any indication as to why the application may be relevant to this trust. In fact, the letter admits it is a circular (in paragraph four), and doesn't really make any effort to counter the ill-effects of this in paragraph six. This kind of approach hardly works when mass-mailing members of the public; it certainly won't to grant-making bodies.

The basic tone of this letter is: 'I know this is impersonal to you [the funder], but please rest assured that we don't treat our "special people" this way'. Not the best way of making a funder feel valued and respected!

Example 2 – A wasted opportunity

Here is a letter to a company asking for prizes to be donated for the charity's spring draw. It has certain merits. For example:

- it is a good length
- it recognises the company's desire for publicity
- it tries to tie the charity in with the company by showing a geographical and personnel connection.

10th September

Dear Mrs Higgins

Each year we run an Autumn Draw in order to raise money for the work of *** Charity. The draw is one of our most important sources of income, enabling us to provide vital support, advice and help for the five million or so people of all ages in the UK with ***, including more than 12,000 children. We do this through our 650 branches; groups for young disabled people; hotels and residential homes; and counselling and information services. We have several branches in Merseyside [where the company is based] and many of your customers and staff will have a first-hand knowledge of the disease.

As 1995 is our 50th anniversary, we will be holding a special Golden Anniversary Draw. Suitable prizes will be crucial to its success and as we rely on donations, if you could help us by donating a prize we would be extremely grateful.

We will, of course, acknowledge your generosity through press releases, our own newspaper, What's Going On? (the best-read publication of its type, going to 100,000 people) including a special souvenir edition, and acknowledgement on the 2 million tickets we will have printed (in mid-October).

In our 50th anniversary year, the combined activities of celebration, fundraising and campaigning at all levels will provide *** Charity and its sponsors with a significant boost to public awareness and support. We are planning several major activities that will generate considerable media interest.

> Any help and support you could offer would be greatly appreciated.
>
> Yours sincerely,
>
> *Richard H. Smibbs*
>
> Events & Exhibitions Manager

However, it could be so much better.

Firstly, this should be a very prestigious affair. A major celebratory year, potentially massive publicity across a wide cross-section of the population and lots of branches to ensure that the two million tickets are sold. Yet the letter is written just one month before the tickets are due to be printed. All this could have been sorted out well in advance. Furthermore, the whole thing should have been presented as a major sponsorship opportunity, rather than merely 'please donate a prize'.

Secondly, the funder has no real idea of the kind of prize required. How many are supposed to be awarded? What was given by whom last year? Did the charity have a particular company product in mind?

The letter says that the draw is a key part of the charity's fundraising. So how much does it raise? A lot of money, no doubt. Again, this could be a real selling point because at little cost to the company (missing out on one sale) the donation could help generate a massive amount of money. This could show terrific leverage.

There are some presentation problems. The first paragraph is very long and rather uninspiring. Why don't they get a user to say how wonderful the charity is or sign up a celebrity appeal patron to say the same thing – anything which makes the appeal a bit more exciting.

The third paragraph offers the company a range of benefits. Because they are all crammed into one sentence, they get a bit lost. Why not separate them out into bullet points?

The point of the fourth paragraph is not clear. Is the charity trying to offer the company further sponsorship opportunities? If so, what are they? Also, what is the centre-piece of the year of celebration (royal visit or whatever)? A carrot could be dangled about this.

Example 3 – Just because you've got problems …

One of the key ideas in this book is that fundraising is about building confidence in the mind of the donor that your plans and ideas are worthwhile and that you can deliver the intended results. Therefore, the best fundraising is usually planned well ahead.

In reality, this is not always possible, and crisis fundraising has its place. However, even here the basic rules stay the same. You are still trying to build confidence in the mind of the donor that whatever has gone on in the past, the future remains bright and that you have sensible plans to get the organisation back on its feet.

Dear Mr Morris

South County Wildlife Trust – Impacts of foot and mouth disease

I am writing to ask for your financial support to help us recover from the impact of Foot and Mouth disease (FMD). Even though the disease has just been announced as being officially cleared, the Trust is still suffering from its disastrous after-effects.

Since its foundation in 1962, the South County Wildlife Trust has become one of the country's most visionary nature conservation charities. Despite being based in the south, many of our projects are recognised as being of national importance. The aim of the Trust is to conserve and protect wildlife habitats and threatened species. This is achieved through the management of nature reserves, the large-scale restoration of rare habitats and by encouraging environmentally sustainable lifestyles through its wide-ranging education programme.

Foot and mouth disease has had serious implications for the South County Wildlife Trust. Ours was one of the first counties to be affected by the disease and much of our work was immediately paralysed. It has been estimated that the Trust will have lost up to one third of its core income as a result of the disease. At the end of this current financial year we are facing a deficit of £150,000 through no fault of our own.

During the summer we were forced to cancel all of our outdoor events, many of which attract the new members we so badly need to

---

support our work. We also had to cancel the 'Murphy Trail', our largest annual fundraising event – a sponsored walk which normally raises over £30,000. This year it raised nothing at all!

In addition, the spread of FMD has set back our conservation work by at least a year. Without access to the countryside we could not check otter holts for signs of habitation, volunteers could not survey rivers for water voles, we could not even put up bird and bat boxes – thus many projects have over-run their scheduled times and budgets.

Replacing lost income, repairing damage to reserves where possible and catching up on our work in the wake of foot and mouth will require extra funds. We have no way of replacing the income we have lost because of the FMD – even our normal fundraising events themselves fell victim to the outbreak.

Our only hope is to ask for your help. The South County Wildlife Trust rarely receives donations in excess of £200 and would therefore greatly welcome any donation to enable us to continue our vital conservation work.

We do hope you will be able to offer your support.

Yours sincerely

S. Cummerford

Fundraising Officer

This application was written at the end of December 2001, in the wake of the Foot and Mouth epidemic that had ravaged many parts of the countryside. There are various flaws in the application, many of which arise out of its introspective nature. Foot and Mouth was not the funder's fault; nor can the medium-sized trust that the application was sent to repair all the damage. Therefore, the application needs to make a convincing case for how it can recover from here. It fails to do this.

Paragraph two makes some typical assertions about how good the organisation is, but without any evidence. You would expect to see at least one example of its 'visionary' work, or allusions to specific projects which are deemed to be of 'national importance'. However, this is somewhat skated over in the rush to get to the key, bad news.

There is no doubt that the wildlife trust has suffered badly through Foot and Mouth, and nobody would seriously dispute that it was not to blame for this. Hence the 'through no fault of our own' is a bit over-stated. The real weakness, however, is not that the application is rather over-written (even though it is), but rather that it does not suggest any constructive way out of the problem.

The critical issue is not that the charity has been unable to raise any money, but that its work has suffered enormously as a result. Again, the application makes a very dangerous assumption, namely that the reader will under-stand all the issues involved. He or she won't. Therefore, why is it a problem that the trust has been unable to put up any bird and bat boxes, or survey the rivers for water voles? How will wildlife suffer as a result? These things need to be pointed out.

Furthermore, you cannot replace a lost year's work all at once. The application needs to be clear about what is the most urgent work that needs doing, and ask for money accordingly. Once that is done they can move on to the next piece. Also, they could even argue for help simply to get the fundraising back on track. Clearly they have been very successful in the past, but may well need extra investment to restore their fundraising strength.

As it stands the application basically reads: 'Help, we're desperate and it's not our fault!' To which the reply is something like: 'I'm sure you are and I'm sure it's not – but what are you actually going to do?' It is often the case that the times you are most in need of money are when you need to be at your most reassuring. Yes, you may have a problem and it may be serious; but you need to show a good, solid, deliverable plan to deliver a brighter future. This application fails to do this, even though the organisation clearly has an awful lot going for it.

Example 4 – Still say what you want

This is a very good application from an excellent project. It clearly meets a need and is a really good example of local people helping regenerate local communities. Being critical, it is rather densely written and a bit repetitive. Some parts, such as the paragraph on the Community Legal Service being awarded a kite mark, could be dealt with much more quickly – in this case in a sentence or two. Getting the award is a good achievement, and helps build credibility, but that is all the application need say on the point.

19th December

Dear Mr Evans

We are writing to ask whether you might be able to assist us with grant aid.

Northtown Neighbourhood Advice Centre was established in 1986 to provide a free, confidential and independent service to the people of Northtown on a wide range of welfare rights issues, e.g. benefits, debt, housing, consumer rights. We offer advice in a variety of ways, (e.g. drop-in, appointments, home visits, telephone, letter, fax) thereby enabling us to give an extremely comprehensive and flexible service. The work of the Centre is primarily concerned with the alleviation of poverty and the issues surrounding deprivation and social exclusion. We are the only advice service in Northtown and one of the few in North County to offer drop-in sessions, which ensures that no client has to wait for more than two days to obtain advice/information. Last financial year we dealt with 5,168 clients and 12,853 queries (an 11% increase on the previous year).

The Centre is very much a community-based project and is managed by a local voluntary Management Committee. A large proportion of the local community relies upon the Centre for an extensive range of invaluable advice and information. The Centre has enormous support from the local community and is seen as a vital resource in a severely deprived area, which has high numbers of unemployed, disabled and elderly people. North County Council and government surveys have shown North County to rank as one of the most deprived areas in the UK with the poorest health in the country. Reliance on incapacity benefit is double the national average and morbidity and standard mortality rate data reveal that people die earlier in North County and suffer longer-term limiting illness than most other areas of the country. The prevalence of disability in North County is three times higher than the national average. The closure of the Centre, due to lack of funds, would deny thousands of vulnerable people the right to a service they so desperately need.

Northtown Neighbourhood Advice Centre was awarded Inner Area Partnership funding in 1986 for a period of six years. The central government funding reached the end of its taper in 1992 leaving us reliant on local authority funding. Since then North County Council have provided us with core funding but we have been dependent upon top-up funding from charities to maintain this service at full strength. We have established a strategy of fundraising in three year periods. This reduces the time spent on fundraising and enables the Workers to focus on client-based work thereby concentrating on providing advice and information and ensuring the project runs smoothly and efficiently. This provides the Centre with the security it needs and ensures continuity of the service to our clients.

We were delighted to move to much larger, more appropriate and accessible premises in December 1997. The premises were afforded to us rent-free by a local company which sadly went into receivership this year. We have raised two grants totaling £31,000 to purchase the property in order to retain the service in these premises, which are ideally located. Unlike the previous arrangement we now have additional costs for building insurance, running costs and maintenance.

We expanded the Service in July 2000 by employing a part-time Administration Worker. The Project was keen to employ a person who lived locally and we were fortunate enough to recruit a highly qualified Administration Worker from Northtown who very quickly became an invaluable team member and an integral part of the service. This essential post ensures the smooth running of the project, the continued employment of a local person and allows the Advice Team to focus on advice giving.

Over the past year there has been a significant change in the advice and information sector. The Community Legal Service launched in April 2000 aims to improve access for the public to quality information, advice and specialist legal services. It comprises a set of standards designed to ensure that a service is well run and has its own quality control mechanisms. In anticipation of the application process, the Centre undertook a full internal audit in which we reviewed all practice and procedure. This resulted in further development of the service and a commitment to review the project annually to ensure that we are meeting our clients' needs and maintaining our commitment to quality. The Centre was awarded the quality mark in August 2001.

The enclosed budget for 2002/2003 is based on the last audited accounts for 2000/2001, the actual expenditure for the first six months of 2001/2002 and an estimation of the final six months of 2001/2002 adjusted to take into account a yearly 3% margin for inflation for the year 2002/2003 and for each subsequent year. We have received a grant from the local authority since the Centre opened in 1986 and we therefore feel fairly assured of our core funding over this period (and have assumed a yearly rise of 3%). We have already raised £30,000 (£10,000 per year for 3 years) from the Greggs trust.

We need to raise the amount shown on the attached budget and are applying to a number of funding bodies. If you are unable to award the total amount, a contribution towards it would be invaluable.

We can provide you with copies of our Annual Report and full audited accounts for 2000/2001 if required (we have not automatically enclosed these due to the cost of reproducing them). Please contact us on our ex-directory number if you would like this or any other additional information.

We hope you will treat our application sympathetically and look forward to your reply. Thank you for your help.

Yours sincerely

Alex Janis

PP. B. Matthews

Chair of the Management Committee

However, the application illustrates very well three common mistakes. Firstly, it is unnecessarily downbeat about its financial achievements. It has an excellent history of obtaining and retaining statutory funding. Rather than the slightly negative 'leaving us reliant on local authority funding' it would read much better to say 'we have successfully secured significant, and growing, local authority funding for over ten years [or whatever]'. This is a really good achievement and should be trumpeted. Many organisations are applying effectively to replace lost statutory funding; this one has maintained and developed it.

The application similarly underplays its fundraising success. Again, the negativity of having to secure 'top-up funding' could be transformed into outlining how the organisation has developed a range of new initiatives (such as the Community Legal Service) or invested in service delivery (for example through the Administrator). They have successfully fundraised for their own building. All this is very impressive, but doesn't come over that well.

Secondly, the application is confusing about money. In fact, the project has already raised 80% of what it needs, so is a long way down the fundraising road. It should be explicit and upbeat about this. This kind of fundraising success breeds confidence and further success. And this should be clearly stated in the application letter rather than the reader having to look elsewhere to find it.

Thirdly, any application should always state what the money will be used for. If the organisation doesn't want to go down a project fundraising road, and they have a strong track record without having done so, they should still say what are the key areas of service delivery they intend to focus on, or who are the key constituencies. It helps give a feeling that the money will be actively used and that there is on-going direction within the organisation.

And finally, never sign an application on behalf of someone else. It looks as if either you couldn't be bothered or that the application is not sufficiently important to wait until you are next in the office. Whatever the reason it leaves a really bad impression.

Example 5 – One thing or the other

This is an appeal from a medical research charity. It realises that it is hard to get wide-scale company money for straight medical research and so, quite rightly, positions this as a public information campaign. However, once again the appeal makes some major mistakes.

Firstly, and fundamentally, it tries to combine two appeals as one. It asks for support both for the postcards to young people and for the GP/health professionals programme. These are two completely different markets. There are a whole range of companies which would be interested in the youth and student market. Are these companies really also going to be interested in GPs? Aren't these the preserve of drugs manufacturers and other health-orientated companies?

One approach may be to put together a really strong, upbeat proposal about new ways of warning of the dangers of the illness. The postcards could work really well, but should be placed in a positive context. The letter's tone suggests 'Oh, it's all very difficult you know'. Why not take the simple line that if people know what to look out for then half the battle is won? Tell a short story about someone who recognised the symptoms early and therefore received quick, successful treatment.

The company needs to be told what they stand to get out of all of this. Where does the proposed £350 fit into the £150,000 total? Why ask the company to pay 0.2% of the required sum? What good does this do? What recognition will the company get out of this?

Why not put together a formal sponsorship proposal based on the postcards? Presumably there will be thousands printed (although this is not stated) and there will be an effective distribution mechanism. The company's logo could be on each card, so would gain it access to a key market. You could even try tying up with a band or night club to get the message better noticed. An alternative to concentrating on the postcards could be to produce a 'wish list' of different publicity options for the company to choose from, each clearly targeted at a particular market.

The GP/health professional leaflet should be an entirely separate proposal, again based on a sponsorship (of the information packs, for example).

Many families in your area have experienced the sudden trauma of *** over the past year. *** is one of the most dangerous of all medical conditions, affecting adults and children alike.

*** Charity is the only major UK charity which focuses solely on the funding of public awareness programmes and vital scientific research as a means to combat *** and which actively involves families affected by the disease in its work.

As you may be aware *** is notoriously difficult to diagnose. Yet with early identification it can often be successfully treated and leaves fewer victims scarred or disabled by their experience. The *** Charity therefore devotes a proportion of its resources to raising public awareness of the signs and symptoms of the disease. There is still a great deal of work that can be done and I hope [company name] will consider supporting the Charity's work. I enclose a copy of the Charity's annual review.

The cases of *** have unfortunately been on the increase with young people. In 1995, there was a two-fold percentage rise in notifications of *** in teenagers and young adults. Currently information resources about these diseases for young adults are scarce and consequently this winter the Charity will launch a specific youth-orientated initiative. Postcards, which are currently used to promote bands and night clubs, will be employed as an accessible medium to promote awareness of the signs and symptoms of *** to young adults. Once produced, the postcards will be distributed to universities, colleges, clubs and restaurants to ensure young adults can access life-saving information on ***.

Another important target group for the winter awareness programme is GP's and health professionals. We aim through the development and distribution of new literature to increase understanding of *** that often accompanies *** and is responsible for the majority of deaths.

To ensure the awareness programme is effective, we need financial backing. Greater public and professional awareness of *** will save lives. In the past companies have been very generous with an average donation of £350. The Foundation is budgeted to spend £150,000 on awareness programmes during the 1996/97 financial year. If you require any further information about the awareness campaigns or the research that we are funding, please do not hesitate to contact me.

I look forward to hearing from you in the near future.

Yours sincerely,

Alan Partridge

Fundraising Officer

Also, the company does not need to know about the gradual improvements in a very difficult medical area. It needs to understand the importance of the problem and that something practical and helpful can be done with its money. The application should describe the PR opportunity rather than simply attempt to sell a medical case.

Finally, there's a strong need for getting an editorial pen to this proposal. Although the above suggestions would change the content quite radically anyway, half the application could effectively be condensed into the following: 'Sadly, the incidence of *** is still on the rise. This is particularly the case with young people (where referrals doubled in 1995). However, the good news is that our researchers show that when people can recognise the symptoms, the number of cases is halved (or whatever). We are launching an exciting new initiative to raise awareness about the disease among young people.' The focus could then move on to the postcards, how wonderfully effective they will be in raising awareness and the terrific publicity opportunity they present.

Example 6 – But what difference would we make?

This letter is from a celebrity. It is generally well-written, if a little long-winded. It certainly makes a compelling case, although no doubt some funders would question some of the statistics (is it really true that only 2% of those involved re-offend? How long after the end of the course were the figures compiled?). Generally the project comes over as being well-run and highly effective. The application contains some basic errors, however, all of which could have been easily avoided.

It's a mail-merged circular. The letter was undated; side two had been pre-printed (including a photocopied signature) onto a roll of computer paper (with the tell-tale perforations top and bottom). So, as a circular it would probably have been binned.

It's a shame that the celebrity didn't actually sign the letter. She is well-known and greatly respected for her community involvement and a personally signed letter from her would give the appeal tremendous weight.

The PS is problematic on two grounds. Firstly, these kinds of PS are best suited to direct mail, and its presence reinforces the impression of a mass mailing rather than a personal letter. Secondly, it suddenly introduces a negative tone, very much out of keeping with the rest of the letter. Why say that the whole future 'is at stake'? It creates doubt in the mind of the donor. If the work is as successful as the letter makes out, there is every reason to assume that the project will go from strength to strength. Try to inspire people to give money, not emotionally bribe or frighten them.

There is also a problem with the way the letter asks for money. Firstly, there is confusion. Are they asking for part of the £500,000 (which is presumably mainly capital expenditure, although this is not clear) or do they want the donor to pay for individual young people at £1,500 a year? They should ask for one or the other, but not both.

In the past you have generously supported the work of *** Foundation, for which we are deeply grateful. Your kindness has allowed over 1,000 people to complete the *** Foundation course, and the results have been remarkable.

I know what it is to plumb the depths of despair. But you don't have to go through what I went through for despair and apathy to take over. Apathy is a problem and it is a killer. It numbs the senses and crushes the spirit. It suffocates self-esteem, blights hope, freezes compassion. Apathy is the product of defeat, and people in our non-functioning inner cities know all about defeat. Many of them are third generation unemployed. Any dreams of success or fulfilment they cherished at school are shattered the moment they leave. Is it any wonder that the first steps to cynicism and alienation start at the school gates.

Almost one million young people are unemployed; 2,874,000 people under 19 live in a household dependent on supplementary benefit and 43% of known offenders are under 21.

You may think this sounds like a lost cause, that the possibility of hauling any young person out of so dire an environment is so slight as to be hopeless. Here at *** Foundation we don't believe in hopelessness, we firmly believe that just because someone has never been given hope it doesn't mean they haven't got any.

A recent survey shows that of the young people who undertook *** Foundation course 42% have found full time employment, 47% have returned to education and 100% undertook a community benefit

---

project. Home Office statistics show that young people who first convict at an early age are more likely to continue offending. 65% of young people had admitted to breaking the law before joining *** and after their involvement with us only 2% have re-offended.

We have shown through the remarkable successes we have had with young people who have undertaken our course, that there is hope and a future for today's youth. Yet there is so much for us still to do – existing centres in *** require expansion to deal with ever-increasing numbers that are being referred to us. New centres need to be established – particularly in ***. Services need to be expanded, but all this requires additional funding.

That is why I am writing to you today, to ask if you will support our national appeal, and raise the £500,000 we need, to give hope and aspiration to more of today's youth.

It costs just £1,500 to fund one young person to go on our course – compare that to the £16,000 a year it costs to keep a young person locked up. A gift of £100 today could radically change the course of a person's life.

The sooner we reach our target, the sooner we can provide the vital work that *** Foundation is renowned for, to communities with high unemployment, high crime and low academic achievement. Please give as much as you can so we can provide a future filled with hope and self-worth for more and more people.

I would like to take this opportunity of wishing you a Happy Christmas, from all the members and staff at *** Foundation, and thank you for your support.

Yours sincerely,

Grace Ellington

PS The enclosed letter from Mary, one of our members sums up in her own words the life of despair she was living before she went on the *** course. The future of young people like Mary and that of *** Foundation is at stake. Please help us to secure both.

If you are going for the £500,000-style approach then you need to have raised some of that total privately before going public (the general rule is get about 25% committed by key donors before opening the appeal up more widely). Give the impression that the appeal has bags of momentum already. Also, you would need to show where the money is coming from and how much you expect trusts, companies or whoever to put in. By breaking everything down into smaller units (say giving yourself a target of £20,000 from companies, £40,000 from trusts, £75,000 from fundraising events etc.), you give the impression that (i) the contribution you are asking for in the letter is much more significant, and (ii) the whole thing is much easier.

Alternatively, if you want £1,500 per person a year, why ask for £100? It doesn't even cover one month's costs. Where does this amount come from? If you are approaching companies, why not set up a friends' scheme whereby they notionally adopt one young person. Or have a corporate members' club whereby you try to recruit W gold members, X silver members, Y bronze members and Z ordinary members. Obviously, the amount each pays comes down as you come down the hierarchy and the benefits you offer increase as you go up. If you are doing this, again you will need to get some members signed up in private first. You need to give the impression in your letter that the company stands to miss out if they don't act now.

Finally, the recipient of this letter had never actually funded the project before. The first line therefore makes a pretty bad impression.

Example 7 – Keep up the momentum

This is a new charity which is clearly meeting a need. The application makes an excellent case, but then rather throws it away at the end. There are various pieces of information that could usefully be added, especially on how many of the 13 million people they are currently helping and how many they plan to help in the future, and what they have done with Lottery funding. However, the basic criticism centres on a very common mistake.

January 2002

Dear Alan

Nearly everyone at some point in their life will experience the terrifying symptoms of an anxiety/panic attack. F.U.S.E., a new organisation, has been established to help people who find themselves in this terrifying situation and it has received official recognition by both the Charity Commission and the National Lottery Charities Board.

There are an estimated 13 million people in the UK who are enduring complicated anxiety-based problems such as panic attacks, phobias and obsessive/compulsive disorders. Often sufferers are too ill or afraid to leave their homes and whilst this affects anyone, anywhere, it is especially a dilemma for people in rural areas where there is little or no quick access to local support. You may, or may not, know that the highest rate of suicide occurs amongst farming communities. People, young and old, who live in small villages, are often extremely isolated and this is not conducive to recovery from an anxiety disorder. We are able to help by running Recovery Groups on a teleconference network. A course covers 14 weeks using cognitive and behavioral therapy with a further opportunity to participate in a befriending group afterwards. This helps to establish and support recovery. Also, group members are encouraged to take an active part in the running of the charity by being trained to act as Group Leaders themselves, consequently furthering their own knowledge and helping more fellow sufferers.

Unfortunately, anxiety illnesses know no boundaries and it is apparent that the services F.U.S.E. can provide are becoming an essential commodity in these stressful times. Our charity is totally non-profit making and volunteer based and we are hoping that you will be able to offer financial support to enable this new and forward-looking project to flourish and grow. We are determined to do our best to make this happen and hope you will help.

Yours sincerely

Samantha Taylor

CHAIRPERSON

The application flags up a compelling issue – in this case the high incidence of anxiety illnesses in rural areas – which really grabs the reader's interest. But then it more or less immediately moves away from it and tails off into a generalised 'please help'.

This is, or should be, an excellent example of project fundraising. Anxiety-based illnesses are clearly a wide-ranging problem and a particular need in rural areas. There is a viable solution on offer, although it needs explaining in more detail. It would seem perfectly natural, therefore, for the application to finish off by simply stating how much this rural work currently costs and how much money they need to develop it further.

It should be fairly straightforward to raise the money needed. This is a newish organisation with a quickly established track record. It simply needs to follow through the argument it begins to develop, and have the confidence to ask for what it actually needs. Remember, fundraising is about change, not money. The case for change is half made, and could easily be fully made. The case for money then flows perfectly naturally.

Example 8 – Building on a local connection

This letter from Hammersmith and Fulham Amenity Trust recognises the importance of the local connection and uses an opportunity from the company chairman's publicly-stated concern to start the grants process moving. Because the company is a very large local employer with long historic ties in the borough, the trust is obviously seeking a large grant. To this end, the first step is to build a relationship, rather than ask for a donation. The letter is the first step; then a phone call; then, hopefully, a meeting to discuss how the trust and the company might work in partnership; and only then, an application for support.

To Richard Fuller, Public Relations Manager of Fuller Smith and Turner from the Director of the Hammersmith and Fulham Amenity Trust

Dear Mr Fuller

UK2000 Thames Project – Environmental Improvements

I noted with pleasure that your chairman, Mr Anthony Fuller, represented Fullers at the UK2000 reception aboard the Elizabethan

---

recently on July 28th, as it demonstrated your company's obvious concern for the environment. I am aware of your company's long association with our part of London, particularly the river, and in view of this I hope that we will be able to link up with you in some of our environmental projects.

Hammersmith and Fulham Amenity Trust was established in 1982 to make our borough a brighter and greener place to visit, work or live in and to create training and employment opportunities. The Trust is an independent charity which receives support from a variety of public and private bodies and carries out a wide range of work including landscape gardening, tree planting, and playgrounds combined with our training schemes for local unemployed people, and events such as the Thames Project. Our newsletter, annual report and other publications are designed to inform the public on green issues and promote a better environment.

Our work is initiated by individuals and groups representing residents, schools, housing associations, playgroups, local businesses, health authorities and the Council – all our projects involve local people in their design, implementation and maintenance after completion.

Currently we have a number of projects which your company may wish to support, ranging from improvements to the riverside and canalside, to greening some of the borough's bleaker housing estates, a garden for a home for the elderly, a children's play area, and tree and bulb planting in several locations.

I hope that your company would like to take the opportunity that the Trust presents to become more closely associated with improving the quality of our environment and I will contact you shortly to discuss further details.

Yours sincerely,

R. Miller

(annual report and newsletter enclosed)

Example 9 – More than a good project

Dear Sir

I am writing to you on behalf of Rock Park Community Association.

We thought that, as a major local employer, you would be interested in the work that we do. In fact many of the people who benefit from our activities have worked for you in the past.

As you are aware, Rock Park is a medium-sized community situated on the edge of Liverpool. It has a modern community centre where we run our activities. We currently operate a weekly lunch club and various other social activities for the senior citizens of our community. These have been going for several years.

We now want to buy a minibus to enable us to provide a pick-up service for people who currently have difficulty accessing our activities. This would also allow us to organise occasional outings to local places of interest.

Our activities are very popular and give opportunities for people to meet and socialise. We have already raised half the money needed to buy the minibus, and are approaching you to request £5,000. We are confident the remainder will be raised from other local sources.

We would be happy to discuss any benefits to your company that could arise from this support.

Yours faithfully

B Welch

This letter is short and clear and makes the geographical link to the company – although it would be far better to have established who to write the letter to rather than address it 'Dear Sir'.

What it fails to do is to state any actual need for the project. While it operates various seemingly successful activities, no case is made for why these activities should be supported, other than that they are popular and allow people to socialise. Are these people isolated in some way, are opportunities to meet limited, is public transport poor? The answer to these questions may well be yes, but the application leaves us guessing.

There is no mention of how many people currently benefit from the activities, or how many more would benefit with the transport provided.

An approach to a company also needs to be specific about the company. If possible it would have been better to get one of the ex-employees who is now a beneficiary volunteer to write.

Example 10 – Stressing the benefits

I am writing to ask for your support for our youth project in Birkenhead.

This project has been running for eight years and was set up following consultations which showed a clear agreement among local residents and agencies that the needs of children and young people present a huge challenge in our area. A survey looking at health and education issues on the estate where the project is based, showed relatively high levels of long-term illness and disability, low educational achievement and high unemployment.

Over the last eight years the project has established regular activities in the community centre on the estate. There are weekly groups for children and young people, as well as activities for families. The local college has run various courses which have proved very popular. Healthy eating courses and parenting courses are also run at regular intervals.

We are aiming to develop this work with young people by setting up a mentoring project. This will cost £12,000 a year for the next three years to employ a part-time co-ordinator. This person's role will be to recruit mentors and match them with young people wishing to benefit from the scheme.

We are working with the Mentoring and Befriending Foundation to ensure the scheme is established in line with best practice and their advice and support has been invaluable.

We will recruit 12 mentors each year who will each meet with a young person on a regular basis over a year. This will mean that after three years 72 young people will have benefitted from the scheme.

We are asking you to provide half the support we need. The rest has already been promised by a local organisation that has supported us previously.

Yours sincerely

T Clarke

Project Manager

This project clearly makes a good case. It has established itself and appears to be addressing the needs of the community. It lists various activities and states precisely what the new scheme (and therefore what the potential funder's money), will do.

However, it does not give the outcomes of this mentoring scheme, only the numbers who will benefit. It does not state how these people will benefit, nor how the community will benefit. There is no mention of who they are actually mentoring nor to what end. Going further, it does not give any indication as to how any outcomes will be measured. Funders increasingly want to know the actual benefits that will result, not just the activities that will be funded.

If the letter had stated the outcomes for the existing work and how they were evaluated, that would give a good indication that the organisation would do it with this new project.

Nothing is mentioned about the mentors themselves — are they from under-represented or hard-to-reach groups? If so, this may add value to the application.

11

Assessing your application

Few applications are perfect, even the ones that raise lots of money. Most can be significantly improved, and it is surprising how many miss out something of real importance.

Before you send off your application, it's worth checking it thoroughly, not just for spelling mistakes, but to make sure that all the details are correct and that you haven't missed out your key selling point or a vital piece of information.

This chapter aims to help you assess:

- How good is your application?
- How, if at all, might you improve it?

Have you written a good application?

Style

- ✔ **The title**: is the project title succinct, catchy, appropriate?
- ✔ **First paragraph**: does the first paragraph grab the reader's attention, create sufficient interest for the reader to continue with the proposal?
- ✔ **Writing**: are you happy with the way you have written this proposal? Does it read well?
- ✔ **Length**: is it the right length? Does it include all the key points you wish to make?

✔ **Tone**: is the proposal positive, confident, enthusiastic? Does it create a sense of urgency and importance for the project?

✔ **Logical flow**: is there a logical structure to the proposal going from problem to solution, from solution to the resources required to provide that solution, and from the resources you require to how the donor can help?

✔ **Visual impression**: is the proposal nicely laid-out with shortish paragraphs, sub-heads and tabulations (where appropriate)? Is it typed neatly and without spelling mistakes?

✔ **Letterhead**: are you happy with your organisation's letterhead? Is it visually attractive? Does it contain all the information it should?

Communication with the donor

✔ **Personal approach**: does the application give the impression of being a personal letter individually written to the donor? Is it signed personally?

✔ **Previous contact**: does the application mention previous approaches or any other contacts you may have had with the donor?

✔ **Donor interests**: is the proposal likely to be of interest to the donor, knowing what you do about their concerns and priorities?

✔ **Donor guidelines**: if the donor publishes guidelines for applicants, have you read these carefully, and does your application fall clearly within the guidelines?

✔ **Scale of request**: is your request reasonable, given what you know about the donor's scale of grant-making?

✔ **Rationale**: have you given good reasons why the donor should want to support the project? If writing to a company, have you clearly stated the benefits they will get from supporting you?

✔ **Empathy**: are you on the same wavelength as the donor? Or, if you are not, does the application build a bridge between your point of view and theirs?

✔ **Signatory**: is the signatory to the letter the most appropriate for the particular donor? And is he or she the first point of contact?

✔ **Follow up**: do you suggest any follow-up if the proposal is of particular interest (a site visit, the supply of further and more detailed information, a meeting)?

✔ **Report back**: if you are seeking substantial support, do you indicate how and at what intervals you intend to report on progress?

. . . or a bad application?

Style

✗ **First paragraph**: is the first paragraph a turn off? Will the reader lose interest and read no further?
✗ **Writing**: is it dreary, verbose and stuffed with jargon, unsubstantiated superlatives, long sentences and unnecessarily long words?
✗ **Length**: is it over-long? Can you shorten it by cutting out unnecessary words? Have you tried to say too much?
✗ **Tone**: is the tone of the proposal hectoring or over-assertive? Is it whinging or apologetic? Or is it complacent?
✗ **Logical flow**: is the application a complete muddle? Do you dart from one point to another and back again? Do you repeat yourself?
✗ **Visual impression**: is the typing a mess? Are there spelling mistakes? Does it contain great chunks of unbroken text?
✗ **Letterhead**: have you got a massive letterhead which takes up half a page? Does it include out-of-date information (e.g. names of trustees who have moved on, are no longer MPs or whatever)? Is there any other problem with it?

Communication with the donor

✗ **Personal approach**: is the application a circular appeal? Does it give the impression of having been sent off to a large number of people (whether or not this is actually the case)?
✗ **Previous contact**: have you failed to mention any previous contact (even if you were turned down)?
✗ **Donor interests**: does the proposal fall completely outside the donor's known concerns and priorities? If so, why are you writing to them (you must have a really good reason)?
✗ **Donor guidelines**: have you forgotten to get hold of the guidelines? Have you not really read them, or deliberately misinterpreted them so that you fit in?
✗ **Scale of request**: does the scale of your need and your request fail to match the scale of the donor's grant-making? Are you looking for such a large sum that the donor can't really make a worthwhile

contribution? Conversely, are you looking for such a small sum that the donor can't really be bothered?

✗ **Rationale**: do you just hope the donor may be interested, that by osmosis they will understand the benefits of their support?

✗ **Empathy**: are you too radical or not radical enough, too establishment or not enough, on the wrong network or wavelength?

✗ **Signatory**: has the application letter been signed by the fundraising assistant, or signed on behalf of the signatory by their secretary? Does this give the impression that you can't really be bothered?

✗ **Report back**: will they next hear from you when you next want money?

Have you written a good application?

Content

✔ **Need**: have you made a good case (centred on your users) and supported it with a few relevant facts and figures?

✔ **Credibility**: have you established that your organisation has the ability, skills and resources necessary to make an impact?

✔ **The proposal**: have you explained in clear, simple terms exactly what you propose to do? Is it backed up by evidence? Is everything the donor needs to know included in the letter?

✔ **Project idea**: is the project likely to be seen as interesting, relevant, attractive to a donor? Does it have the support of users? Will it bring measurable benefits to the lives of your users?

✔ **Objectives**: have you set yourself specific and measurable objectives for the project? And are these reasonable given the level of staff time and resources at your disposal? Are you confident?

✔ **Outcomes**: have you clearly defined the outcomes for the project? Do they clearly meet the identified need? Have you shown how they will be measured?

✔ **Evaluation**: do you intend to evaluate the outcome of your work and have you shown how you intend to set about doing this? Is this likely to be effective and is it being done at reasonable cost?

✔ **Dissemination**: if the proposal is for a pilot project, for research or action research, or to produce a publication, have you shown how you plan to disseminate the results, or what you have produced with the grant?

✔ **The offer**: have you made a specific request for support or given a clear indication to the donor as to how much you want them to give? Have you mentioned where the rest of the money is coming from, or who has already given to the appeal?

✔ **Future funding**: have you at least shown that you have thought about the future funding implications of the proposal (the running costs, or whatever) even though there may be no certain answers at this stage?

Budget

✔ **Arithmetic**: do the figures add up?

✔ **Costings**: have you included all the items of expenditure that you plan to incur? Are all the items costed realistically?

✔ **Overheads**: where appropriate, have you included an apportionment of overhead or administrative costs in your budget? Does the basis on which you have calculated this appear reasonable?

✔ **Value**: does the total cost appear to be reasonable in relation to the work you plan to do? Does the proposal represent value for the donor's money? Is this clear from what you have said?

✔ **Inflation**: if the project is to run over several years, have you made any allowance for inflation (or stated that the budget for future years does not take account of any inflation in costs)?

Supporting information

✔ **Finance**: have you included your annual accounts and a budget for the project?

✔ **Brochure**: have you got a suitable brochure or report to attach? Does it enhance what you say in the application? Is it nicely designed and illustrated?

✔ **Other**: is there any other information you could or should include?

. . . or a bad application?

Content

✗ **Need**: have you simply assumed that everyone knows what you are doing is important? Have you spoken in generalisations and made bland assertions?

✗ **Credibility**: have you assumed that everybody has heard about you, thinks well of you, and is convinced of your capabilities?

✗ **Proposal**: is your description of the project muddled? Incomplete? Are you expecting the donor to wade through loads of supporting material to get a proper idea of what you are trying to do.

✗ **Project idea**: have you made the project seem boring, old-fashioned, of marginal benefit?

✗ **Objectives**: have you failed to set objectives? Are they very generalised, couched in 'We hope this. . .' or 'We may do. . .'? Or are the objectives so grandiose that they become completely unrealistic?

✗ **Outcomes**: are your outcomes unclearly defined? Is the relationship between the need and the outcome clear? Are the outcomes immeasurable?

✗ **Dissemination**: are you keeping everything to yourselves?

✗ **The offer**: have you mentioned some global fundraising target and simply asked for 'a generous contribution'? Have you given no indication of the scale of support you are looking for?

✗ **Future funding**: are you asking for running costs and not indicating how the project will continue in future years? Are you asking for an item of equipment or raising money for a building, without giving any indication of how the running costs will be met?

Budget

✗ **Arithmetic**: are there silly mistakes in your addition?

✗ **Costings**: have you forgotten to include certain items of expenditure? Are the figures just 'plucked out of the air'? Have you obtained any quotes or estimates for larger items of capital expenditure?

✗ **Value**: does the proposal seem a lot of money for your plans?

Supporting information

✗ **Brochure**: is your supporting material written for internal consumption (as, say, a discussion document)? Is it written in long paragraphs, no sub heads, heavily jargonised? Is it overly glossy or does it look too cheap?

Assessing your application

Now assess your application on the following lines:

Factor	Satisfied?	Action points
Style	Yes/no	
Title		
First paragraph		
Writing		
Length		
Tone		
Logical flow		
Visual impression		
Letterhead		
Communication with donor	Yes/no	
Personal approach		
Previous contact		

Factor	Satisfied?	Action points
Donor interests		
Donor guidelines		
Scale of request		
Rationale		
Empathy		
Signatory		
Follow up		
Report back		
Content	Yes/no	
Need		
Credibility		
Proposal		
Project idea		
Objectives		
Outcomes		
Evaluation		
Dissemination		
The offer		
Future funding		

Factor	Satisfied?	Action points
Budget	Yes/no	
Arithmetic		
Costings		
Overheads		
Value for money		
Inflation		
Supporting information	Yes/no	
Finance		
Brochure		
Other		

12

Checklists and fact files

Serious fundraising requires serious record-keeping. Much of this involves getting information that is dispersed throughout the organisation (or lives only in people's heads) and putting it into a central file. This can be time-consuming. However, once you have done it (and as long as you keep updating it as you go) it is a fairly straightforward maintenance job.

The information you keep is entirely up to you. The following covers the various points and issues discussed in this book. Use it or adapt it as necessary.

Contents

1 Organisation fact file

The basic facts about your organisation, its aims and its history. Often this is forgotten.

2 Credibility fact file

Some basic information about the successes and achievements of the organisation, its main financial sponsors (whose support provides an endorsement) and note of any recent press and media coverage.

3 Credibility box file

A box file in which you keep endorsements; quotations; lists of patrons and financial sponsors; clippings from newspaper articles or research reports highlighting the problem or need; statistics and trends which demonstrate the full extent of the problem and how the situation is changing; evaluation reports which reflect the good work being done by the organisation; case studies and photographs that put a human face on your work; in fact anything that might be useful in reinforcing your case. Every organisation should have one!

4 Fundraising plan for the organisation

To help you plan your fundraising needs well in advance.

5 Project fact file

The basic facts about your project, its importance and how it will be run.

6 Budget checklist

To help you plan your expenditure requirements.

7 Fundraising plan for the project

To help you plan where and how you will raise the money you need for your project, and to develop contingency plans if you are not immediately successful.

8 Keeping track of progress

Checklists to record the grants and donations you receive and to track the progress of your more important applications.

9 Mobilising contacts

To help you identify the personal contacts and mobilise the support of your staff, trustees, patrons and others who can help you in your fundraising.

1 Organisation fact file

Last updated:

Name of your organisation:

Address:

Date founded:

Why, how and by whom founded:

Key events in your organisation's history (up to 5):

Charitable status:
 Registration or reference no:

 If not a charity, describe status of the organisation:

 VAT registration no:

People involved
 numbers of full time staff: numbers of part time staff:
 numbers of volunteers: volunteer hours a year:
 individual membership: institutional membership:

Annual income
 total income:
 total raised from grants and donations:
 total self-generated:
 total expenditure:
 total assets:

Mission statement:

Principal objects or purposes of the organisation:

Present policies and priorities:

Business plan last updated in:

Beneficial area or area over which the organisation operates:

Affiliations with other relevant organisations:

The organisation: what makes it unique or different and why its work is especially important (3 key facts):

Recent growth in the organisation and in the demand for its services (3 key statistics):

2 Credibility fact file

Last updated:

List your five greatest successes in the past five years:

Other recent successes and achievements of the organisation (2 or 3):

Main financial sponsors:
- government and other official sources:

- grant-making trusts:

- business sponsors:

- individual supporters:

- prominent patrons and supporters:

Recent press or media coverage:

3 Credibility box file

This is simply where you keep all the press coverage, statements, quotations, evaluations or other information about the organisation which endorse the value of its work. Once it's full, start pruning the out-of-date clippings.

4 A fundraising plan for the organisation

Fundraising always takes time, and it is sensible to plan well ahead. Ideally draw up a three- or five-year budget of income and expenditure. The following is a suggestion for an income budget in order to plan your fundraising (an expenditure budget in this book would be so generalised as to be useless).

Start by looking at your income and expenditure over the last four or five years. Do you notice any trends (e.g. rise in salary or premises costs; fall in local authority grant; growth in income from grant-making trusts; increasing reliance on one source of income)? Make a note of them and make sure your fundraising plan takes full account of them. For example, if you have never had any company sponsorship, it will take time to build this up. Don't put £100,000 down in year one just because it looks good.

When compiling your figures, make a note of any assumptions and action points, particularly with regard to large chunks of income. Also, remember that this exercise is, at best, a guesstimate. You cannot guarantee future income, so if it appears you have got your projections wrong, change them.

Finally, be honest and realistic! The temptation is to write up income and write down expenditure, when it is more often the other way round.

Here are some possible budget headings you might use for your income projections.

Total budgeted or estimated expenditure for the year £ _____

Income to be raised (by category)
    Investment income and bank interest   £ _____

    Earned income from:
        contracts for service delivery   £ _____
        other sale of services   £ _____
        training & conferences   £ _____
        publication sales   £ _____
        other trading activities   £ _____

    Grants/payments from:
        central government   £ _____
        local government   £ _____
        other statutory sources   £ _____
        trusts   £ _____
        National Lottery   £ _____
        company donations   £ _____
        business sponsorship   £ _____
        other sources   £ _____

Public fundraising

    membership subscriptions   £ _____

    fundraising events   £ _____

    Gift Aid/planned giving   £ _____

    collections   £ _____

    other   £ _____

Legacies   £ _____

Total income budgeted for the year   £ _____

Budgeted surplus or deficit   £ _____

Comments

Key dates:

    schedule of expiring grants:

        larger grants which are likely to be renewed (list sources/annual amount/expiry date/renewal action to be taken and by whom/comments)

        larger grants which are unlikely to be renewed (list sources/annual amount/expiry date/suggestions for alternative sources of funding/comments)

    schedule of expiring contracts/service agreements:

        major contracts/service agreements which are likely to be renewed

        major contracts/service agreements which are unlikely to be renewed

    key fundraising events (timetable for who is doing what and by when)

    covenant/Gift Aid tax reclaim (who does it by when)

5 Project fact file

This brings together information about the project you are raising money for

Last updated:

Description of the proposed project/purpose of the application (not more than 20 words):

The need for the project – 3 key facts:

Evidence that users believe that there is a need:

Partner organisations (how and why are they involved):

Why it is so important to undertake the project at the present time (3 key points):

The objective (main aim) of the project:

How and when will the above objective come about (specific and measurable outputs and outcomes)?

Methods which will be used to undertake the project:
Up to five key tasks you will undertake in the first year:

User involvement: how will the users be involved in the work?

Volunteer inputs: how are volunteers to be involved and what is the value of this?

How do you plan to disseminate any results or the outcome of the project?

How will the project be evaluated?

Any consequences or anticipated future impact which will result from the project:

Estimated start date of the project:

Estimated completion date or term of the project:

Key people involved and relevant experience:

Outside advisers:

Any other details of the project which are particularly special or noteworthy:

6 Budget checklist – revenue project

Here is an outline budget for a revenue project. We have left space at the bottom for two subsequent revisions, the first in the light of your assessment of the fundraising potential of the project (you may wish to increase or reduce certain costs, or add to or subtract from the project), and the second to allow you to confirm or get better estimates for the major items of cost.

Project title:

1st draft

	Year 1	Year 2	Year 3
Employment costs/salaries (inc. National Insurance)	....	....	....
Recruitment costs	....	....	....
Volunteer expenses/ training costs	....	....	....
Project costs			
Equipment	....	....	....
Printing/stationery	....	....	....
Post/telephone	....	....	....
Travel/transport	....	....	....
Training	....	....	....
Evaluation	....	....	....
Technical advice/ consultancy	....	....	....
Dissemination of results	....	....	....
Other project costs	....	....	....
	....	....	....
	....	....	....

	Year 1	Year 2	Year 3
Overhead costs *			
Office occupancy (rent/rates/heat/ light etc.)	....	....	....
Management & administration	....	....	....
Central services (cleaning etc.)	....	....	....
Depreciation	....	....	....
Other overhead costs	....	....	....
	....	....	....
	....	....	....
TOTAL	£...............	£...............	£...............

* State basis on which overhead costs have been apportioned to the project

State basis on which inflation has been allowed for in the second and third years

State any other relevant assumptions

		Year 1	Year 2	Year 3
First revision	TOTAL	....	....	....
Second revision	TOTAL	....	....	....

7 Fundraising plan for the project

Just as you will need an income budget for the organisation, you will also need budgets for each of the projects that the organisation undertakes as part of its work. Having costed the project – (see Checklist 6 Budget checklist), you will need to draw up an income budget. You will need a separate column for each year of the project.

Firstly, categorise the budgeted income under the different heads:

- government and other statutory sources
- grant-making trusts and other charities
- business support (inc. sponsorship and gifts in kind)
- donations from members/individual supporters
- fundraising events and activities
- your organisation's own contribution
- other

Under each income source, you will need to list:

- total income to be raised from that source
- a list of grants raised or committed to date, and a total for this committed income
- a list of likely grants still being negotiated or decided, and a total for this probable income
- the total income still required
- any notes or comments

Compare your Fundraising plan for the project with Checklist 4 A Fundraising plan for the organisation. For example, are you aiming to use the entire trust's budget for a single project? If so, (i) is this realistic, and (ii) what about the other projects you are trying to raise money for?

You will need to keep your project plan up-to-date, recording grants when they come in and revising estimates and running totals accordingly. Where you fail to secure a major grant which you had been planning for, you may need to revise your whole approach. A contingency plan can alert you to the possibilities.

8 Keeping track of progress

You need to keep track of the progress of each key grant you have applied for. In the light of this, review the situation regularly and take action sooner rather than later. If you don't, you may end up with a large hole in your budget. For each grant, keep the following information:

Who you applied to

How much you asked for/expect

Name of person you sent it to

Who signed the letter

Date application was sent off

Expected decision date

Follow up action:
   (i) action already taken

   (ii) the possibilities of further action

   (iii) suggestions for possible alternative sources

Person responsible for negotiating the grant

9 Mobilising contacts

You can improve your chances significantly by developing good personal contacts with the trustees and others responsible for grants decisions in the bodies you are approaching. This section provides an 'audit' of the contacts that you, your colleagues, your trustees and your patrons already have as a start to mobilising their support. Remember too that your employee volunteers can be particularly important when approaching their employer.

For each of your colleagues, your trustees, your patrons, and possibly even some of your key supporters and most committed volunteers, keep a record of the following information.

Name

Position/occupation

Contact address/phone/fax/e-mail

Any relevant skills they have and help they are prepared to give

Useful contacts they are prepared to approach for support (or let you approach on their behalf)

   Name/position/address/telephone of the contact

Funding body and their connection with it

Whether you or they will make the approach

Notes (e.g. what is the existing relationship with this contact/funding body)

The help you will want from your supporters will be anything from:
- Sounding the funder out
- Having a quiet, informal word over dinner
- Attending (or even making) a formal presentation of your project to the funder
- Signing a covering letter
- Asking formally for money face to face

For further information see *Data Protection for Voluntary Organisations*, Paul Ticher, published by DSC.

Further reading and sources of information

About the Directory of Social Change

DSC has a vision of an independent voluntary sector at the heart of social change. The activities of independent charities, voluntary organisations and community groups are fundamental to achieve social change. We exist to help these organisations and the people who support them to achieve their goals.

We do this by:

- providing practical tools that organisations and activists need, including online and printed publications, training courses, and conferences on a huge range of topics
- acting as a 'concerned citizen' in public policy debates, often on behalf of smaller charities, voluntary organisations and community groups
- leading campaigns and stimulating debate on key policy issues that affect those groups
- carrying out research and providing information to influence policy-makers.

DSC is the leading provider of information and training for the voluntary sector and publishes an extensive range of guides and handbooks covering subjects such as fundraising, management, communication, finance and law. We have a range of subscription-based websites containing a wealth of information on funding from trusts, companies and government sources. We run more than 300 training courses each year, including bespoke in-house training provided at the client's location. DSC conferences, many of which run on an annual basis, include the Charity Management Conference, the Charity Accountants' Conference and the Charity Law Conference. DSC's major annual event is Charityfair, which provides low-cost training on a wide variety of subjects.

For details of all our activities, and to order publications and book courses, go to: www.dsc.org.uk, call 08450 777707 or email publications@dsc.org.uk

Resources available from DSC

The following is a selection of resources available from DSC.

Telephone us on 08450 77 77 07 or email publications@dsc.org.uk for a complete publications or training catalogue, or visit the DSC website: www.dsc.org.uk

Details were correct at the time of going to press but may be subject to change.

Fundraising directories

The Directory of Grant Making Trusts, published biennially

The Guide to the Major Trusts, Volumes 1 and 2, published biennially

The Guide to UK Company Giving, published biennially

The Guide to Educational Grants, published biennially

The Guide to Grants for Individuals in Need, published biennially

Environment Funding Guide, 4th edn, Denise Lillya

Sports Funding Guide, 3rd edn, Tom Traynor and Denise Lillya

Youth Funding Guide, 3rd edn, Denise Lillya

Fundraising handbooks

The Complete Fundraising Handbook, 6th edn, Nina Botting Herbst and Michael Norton, 2012

Complete Special Events Handbook, Pauline Carter

Effective Fundraising, Luke Fitzherbert

Finding Company Sponsors for Good Causes, Chris Wells

Find the Funds, Christopher Carnie

Looking after your Donors, Karen Gilchrist

Tried and Tested Ideas for Local Fundraising Events, 3rd edn, Sarah Passingham

The Worldwide Fundraiser's Handbook, 3rd edn, Michael Norton

Other fundraising titles

Capital Campaigns, Trudy Hayden

Corporate Fundraising, 4th edn, Valerie Morton (ed.)

Fundraising Databases, Peter Flory

Legacy Fundraising, 2nd edn, Sebastian Wilberforce (ed.)

Major Donor Fundraising, Margaret Holman and Lucy Sargent

Marketing Strategy for Effective Fundraising, Peter Maple

Patrons, Presidents and Personalities, Eileen Hammond

The Porcupine Principle and other fundraising secrets, Jonathan Farnhill

Promoting Your Cause: A guide for fundraisers and campaigners, Karen Gilchrist

Trust Fundraising, Antony Clay (ed.)

Why Rich People Give, Theresa Lloyd

Fundraising websites

www.governmentfunding.org.uk is an online window to funding from local, regional and national government, independent grant administrators as well as European sources.

www.trustfunding.org.uk provides information on more than 4,000 trusts with more added every month.

www.companygiving.org.uk contains all those companies in *The Guide to UK Company Giving* and newly discovered givers.

www.grantsforindividuals.org.uk provides sources of funds for individuals in need and for educational purposes.

Index

accounts 32–4, 65. 100, 101, 119, 137
ACEVO 41, 43–6 *passim*, 53, 61
amount to ask for 4, 79, 95–6, 102,
    103, 124, 126, 128, 134–8 *passim*
application form 1, 3, 78, 82–3
approach, making 5, 102–8; blanket
    103; delayed 105–6; personal 134,
    135; scatter-gun 4, 77; step-by-step
    103–5, 128
assertions 3, 8, 75, 87, 110–11, 115, 138
assessing application 36, 104, 107,
    133–41
attachments 100–1

back-up material 5, 76, 101
BBC Children in Need 78, 88, 104
benefits, to donors 20, 80–1, 97, 113,
    121, 130; to users 8–9, 11, 16–18
    passim, 55, 88–9, 130–2
BIG 16, 25–6, 35, 36, 45, 51, 52, 62, 78,
    80; Reaching Communities
    programme 7, 8, 11, 14, 18, 25–6,
    33, 51
brochures 3, 5, 137, 139, 141
budget 4, 33, 45, 46, 56–65, 93–4, 100,
    101, 119, 137–9 *passim*, 141, 146–8,
    153; checklist 143, 151–2; mistakes
    64–5, 138; stages 57–64

CD-ROM 76
celebrities 12–13, 113, 123
charges 17, 47, 97

Charities Act 99
Charities Evaluation Services 52;
    Planning Triangle 16
circulars 4, 78, 109, 111, 123, 135
collaboration with other organisations
    21, 25
communication skills 66–76; tips 74–5;
    writer's diseases 68–71
Community Fund 14
community, support from 21, 26, 28,
    117
companies 4, 20, 54, 76, 78–81 *passim*,
    97, 100, 113, 120–3 *passim*; budgets
    4, 78
confidence 24, 63, 95, 98, 105; donor
    4, 24, 26, 55, 93, 94, 98, 102, 114
connections, with donors 4, 79, 85, 97,
    112, 128–30 *passim*
consultation 9, 11, 18, 87, 89, 92
contacts, with donors 5, 23, 29, 106,
    134, 135, 143, 155–6
continuation of project 97–8, 118, 137,
    138
contracts 41, 42, 54, 97
conversion, cost/donation 44
correspondent 77, 78, 109, 130
cost-effectiveness 16–17, 19, 36, 47, 83,
    89
costing/costs 4, 16, 17, 33, 41–7, 56–65,
    93–4, 137, 138;
    administration/running 46, 59–62
    passim, 64, 138; core 41–4 *passim*,

60, 61, 118; forgotten/hidden 61, 64;
    overheads 33, 41–6 *passim*, 56,
    60–2, 64, 93, 137, *see also* full cost
    recovery
credibility 2–5 *passim*, 23–34, 49, 86,
    107, 136, 138; box files 142–3, 146;
    fact files 31–2, 142, 145–6

deficits 33, 35, 36, 114
development expenditure 53–4;
    funding 43, 57
directories, fundraising 158–9
Directory of Social Change 157–8
dissemination 55, 137, 138
DVDs 76

effectiveness 2, 13–16, 24, 47, 49, 83
efficiency 19, 24–5, 45, 54
email/fax 75, 76, 78
emergency funding 108, 114–16
endorsements 4, 15, 24, 28, 85, 101,
    102, 105, 142
equal opportunities 36, 110
equipment 54, 60, 95
Esmée Fairbairn Charitable Trust 104
evaluation 14, 15, 17, 18, 28, 49–51,
    91–3, 110, 136, 143
events/open days 81, 105, 153
examples 19–20, 38–9, 50, 57–64,
    109–32
exercises 10, 13, 15, 18, 22, 27, 28, 34,
    48, 72–3
expenditure 4, 32, 40, 45, 46, 53–4,
    58, 60–1, 93, 119, 137, 138, 146,
    147

failure 5, 6, 37–8, 107
feedback 9, 18, 28, 49, 92–3
fees 47; professional 58, 61, 62
follow-up 5, 99, 103, 106–7, 134
friends' scheme 126
full cost recovery 41–7, 56, 60, 61;
    benefits 43–5; *Toolkit* 61

generalisations 8, 11, 87, 138
governance, of organisation 25–6;
    Guide 25–6

grants 41, 46, 47, 54–5, 63, 78, 79, 95,
    96, 98, 153; committee 83, 107;
    cycle 104, 106; matching 54; range
    79, 134, 135
guidelines, donor 5, 82–3, 105, 134,
    135

handbooks, fundraising 159

ideas, good 1, 4, 24, 48, 52–3, 136,
    138
impact 1, 3, 17, 29, 47, 49, 54, 55,
    89
income 46, 54, 59, 97; budget
    146–8, 153; generation 17,
    97–8
inflation 64–5, 94, 119, 137
inputs 12, 14, 50
interest, expression of 5, 80, 83,
    105
interest/priorities, donor 2–4
    passim, 7, 14, 19, 77, 78, 82,
    96–7, 109, 134, 135
introductions, to patrons etc. 81
investment 53–4

jargon 68, 74, 101, 110–11

length, of application 82, 99–100,
    112, 133, 135, 139
letter, application 76, 83–5, 110–32
    passim
letterhead 31, 134, 135, 139
leverage 19, 21, 48, 54–5, 64, 102,
    113
Lloyds TSB 104
local authorities 19, 42, 108, 118,
    119

maintenance 58–9, 118
management committee 13, 18, 21,
    24, 36, 117
mailing, direct 3; mass 111, 123
meetings, with funders 4, 103–5
    passim
membership 21, 98, 126
methods 88–91, 149–50

monitoring 14, 15, 17, 18, 33, 49–51 *passim*, 91–3

NAVCA 52
National Audit Office 45
National Lottery Distribution Boards 80
need 1, 3, 8–12, 19, 22, 48, 52, 83, 86–8, 101, 130, 136, 138; assessment of 11, 86–8; identifying 8–9. 87
non-cash support 1, 20, 26, 27, 32

objectives 5, 15, 16, 37, 48, 49, 88–90, 136, 138
outcomes 4, 8, 13–16 *passim*, 19, 24, 29, 47, 49, 51–2, 55, 88–91, 132, 136, 138; indicators 52, 91; SMART 61–2
outputs 12, 15, 16, 29, 44, 48, 50

partnership 3, 25, 29, 30, 62, 79, 111, 128
patrons 23, 30, 31, 106, 113, 142, 155–6
planning 4, 18, 24, 44, 88, 107
plans, business 38; funding 4, 13, 94–5, 98, 101, 105, 143, 146–8, 153
pledge system 104–5
potential funders 1, 4, 7–8, 30–1, 76, 102–8 *passim*
presentations 1, 76
press coverage 24, 28–9, 101, 112, 142
prizes 112
problems 1, 8–12, 86–91, 101
procedure, application 3, 5, 78–80 *passim*, 83, 104, 105
professionalism 19, 25–6, 28
progress, checklists 143, 154; measuring 49–51; reports 29, 50
projects 40–65; budget 153; costing 4, 33, 41–7, 56–65; evaluation 49–51; fact file 143, 149–50; fundability 47–8; plan 143, 153
proposal 1, 3–22 *passim*, 65, 83–99, 110–32, 136, 138; ingredients 3, 6–22; introduction 85–6, 133, 135;

outline form 5, 80, 105; purpose 5–6, 65; structure 84–99; summary 84–5, 100; title 48, 84, 133
publicity 3, 20, 80, 97, 106, 112, 113, 121, 123

questionnaires 9, 18, 92
'quotes sheet' 28, 101

rationale 7, 21, 96–7, 134, 136
re-approaching 6, 9, 106–7
records 106, 142–56
rejection 5, 106; reasons for 5, 34–5, 103, 106
relationships, building 2–3, 6, 25, 29–30, 107, 108, 128
relevance 47, 51, 111
report, annual 5, 29, 100, 101, 105, 119
reporting 29, 50–1, 65, 81, 134, 136
requirements, donor 5, 49–51, 65, 106
research 2, 8, 9, 11, 121; on donors 4, 77–81
reserves 33, 34
risk 13, 26, 78–9

secondments 27
security 17, 20, 54, 58, 118
selling points 3, 7, 19–22, 133
services 17, 44, 47, 50, 120; agreements 42, 54
shopping list 96
shortfalls 33, 44, 65
signatory 98–9, 111, 120, 134, 136
sponsorship 1, 78, 80, 113, 121, 142, 147
staff 24–6 *passim*, 61, 62, 101
statistics 3, 9, 11, 87, 123, 125, 143
statutory funders 19, 20, 31–2, 97, 104, 108, 117–19
success 3–5, 15, 28, 37, 51, 55, 90, 107, 120, 142
surplus 32, 46
sustainability 20, 41, 45, 59
style 133–6 *passim*

tapering 98, 117

targeting 4, 30, 106

targets (milestones) 49–52 *passim*, 88, 90, 91

technology 54

telephone, use of 1, 29, 76; cold-calling 76

tendering 44

thanking 5, 29, 81, 106

timing 107–8

topicality 47, 48

topping up 103, 118, 120

track record 13–15 *passim*, 24, 26, 37, 93, 94, 120, 128

training 25, 54, 62

Treasury 41–2

trustees 21, 23, 25, 30, 31, 61, 101, 106, 107, 155–6

trusts 16, 19–20, 35, 45, 78–80 *passim*, 83, 100, 102, 104

Tudor trust 83

TV/radio coverage 29

under-costing 56, 64–5

users 2, 8–9, 11, 16, 17, 26, 52, 58, 86–9; involvement 2, 18–20, 26, 36, 89, 92

value, adding 53–5

value for money 16–17, 21, 47, 48, 53–5, 80, 89, 137, 138

verbicide 68

verbification 71

verbitis 68–9

verbosity 69–70

videos 76

visits, by funders 1, 28, 29, 103, 105

volunteers 18, 20, 25–7 *passim*, 32, 55, 61, 155–6; involvement 20

weaknesses 34–9; dealing with 38

websites 31, 76, 160

word processing 76